D1616266

Getting To Scratch

Practical advice and application to help you
lower your golf scores

Lewis M. Greer

Getting To Scratch
Copyright © 2015 by Lewis M. Greer

For information or inquiries, visit www.dogoodbooks.com

ISBN: 978-0-9712723-6-1

Published by Do Good Books

First electronic edition, May, 2015. First printing, July, 2015
10 9 8 7 6 5 4 3 2 1

FOR BILL AND GEORGE GREER

There have been better golfers,
but never a better brother or father.

Table of Contents

I only like certain golf books. Golf instruction books that are too technical and deep put me to sleep. Other golf books, like Harvey Penick's popular seller *Little Red Book; Lessons and Teachings from a Lifetime in Golf,* and the book you are reading now, inspire, teach, and make golf fun. Lewis Greer has hit a 300 yard drive right down the middle of the fairway with *Getting to Scratch.*

It is basic, good information about golf and life and is written with humor and great insight. I would expect nothing less from Lewis Greer. He writes like he lives life. Lewis is sensible, perceptive, and always has a touch of humor and humility. I have always found him to be well grounded in life and in his faith in Jesus. Both become evident when you read this book.

Some time back a writer said, "Golf is the most taught, least learned human endeavor in the whole spectrum of doctrinology. If we taught sex the way we teach golf, the race would have died out years ago." Golf needs to be taught the way Lewis writes this book, filled with psychological lessons, simple common sense instruction, good stories, and positive thinking.

Read on and be refreshed. I desire to spend the balance of my golf life with golf truths that make sense like his chapter on Perfection. Lewis states "This will be a fairly short chapter, but coming right after 'Doubt' is a good place for it. Here is something you should never doubt: you cannot achieve perfection in golf."

If you want to enjoy golf and life more and learn some simple truths to help you in the delight of both, this is the perfect book for you.

Randy Wolff, former PGA Tour player

INTRODUCTION

If you've played much golf at all you've heard the phrase *It's not how, it's how many.* If that is true—and as far as the money and trophies are concerned it seems to be—then why do we use most of our gray cells trying to answer the question of how?

Pick up any golf magazine or video, and the likely focus is how to hit shots. Longer drives, solid irons, delicate chips, perfect putts, bunker shots, fades, draws, high-and-soft, low-and-running—you name it and there is an article about how to hit it.

The thinking goes, of course, that if you learn how to hit all of those shots your score will go down. Maybe it will, and maybe it won't.

Take distance on your drives as an example. Most every player in the game (and this includes me) would like to hit the ball longer than they do—especially off the tee—even though it has been proven over and over that the longest hitters are not necessarily the biggest winners. Yes, long-hitting Bubba Watson has two Masters titles, but short-hitting Corey

Pavin and Tom Kite each won a U.S. Open. Distance can be an advantage, but it can also be a trap. More about that later.

"Ah," you say, "then it must be about hitting greens in regulation." Nope.

Examine the stats from the PGA Tour for the last few years, and you'll see that the leader in that category is often far from being the biggest winner. In fact three of the last four years (as I write), the leader in greens in regulation did not make enough money to maintain his PGA Tour card.

Short game? If you include putting in that category, there is no question that more strokes are added to our scores through poor short-game play than anywhere else. To put a positive spin on it, consider the statistical category called "strokes gained putting," a measure of how well a player putts compared to the field on any given day, week, or up to some point in the season. The leader in that category is often near the top of the money list. Interestingly, the short game, especially putting, is the one part of the game where virtually every professional recognizes individuality in manner and technique.

In other words, from somewhere around the green to on the green, you are allowed to be you and not a clone of an idealized golfer. That is freeing for some and scary for others, but there is an important lesson in it that we will explore.

Stating what may or may not be obvious, the key to lower scores, whether you are playing in a club match or to make a living, is to get the ball in the hole sooner. Longer drives and more accurate irons might help facilitate that, but there is clearly no direct "cause and effect" between having prodigious distance and being a world-beater, nor is there such a relationship with the category known as ball-striking. Even in the all-important disciplines of chipping and putting, how you do those things is not the key.

In these pages we'll go into all of those ideas more deeply, and I'll share lessons with you that will, when applied, lower your scores. Once in a while we may get to the fringe of *how*, but the green we are going for is *how many*.

May your number grow smaller.

1

The Easy Stuff

part one: equipment

Let's begin our golf journey in a pool room. Back when I was in college in southern Illinois (pre-Army) I worked part time in a couple of different pool halls. One was the nice kind, with carpet on the floor, plenty of lights, and even a legitimate billiards table to go with ten pool tables. We also had a counter with a grill behind it, a picture window, and a show table up front that was viewable through the window. Because it was near the door and the grill, that part of the floor was covered with some kind of tile. My job was to collect table fees, cook hamburgers and sweep the floors. Naturally I shot a little pool when the place was not busy.

One day about 2 p.m. I was doing just that when a gold

Cadillac with a black top pulled up in front. Through the picture window I saw a heavy-set man remove himself from behind the wheel and walk toward our door. I thought I recognized him, and then I saw his personalized license plate, which read MF 8.

He came in and asked if the manager was there, and I said he was in the back office. And then the man picked up the broom I'd been using earlier to sweep the tile floor. Wielding the broom handle as a pool cue he made several shots on our front table. Had there been any doubt in my mind about his identity, that was now gone. He really was the legendary Minnesota Fats.

Just as Fats could use a broom better than most pool players could use a custom cue, an excellent golfer can hit quality golf shots with pretty much any golf club. Sam Snead is said to have hit shots with a branch from a tree. But Snead didn't use a branch in tournaments, and Fats didn't use a broom when the game was on. Unless you wanted to bet him that he couldn't run the table with one.

One of the simplest things any golfer can do to shoot lower scores is to use the right equipment. That means personal fitting, and fitting is not just for professionals and low-handicap amateurs. In fact, golfers who shoot between 80 and 95 will probably benefit the most from fitting. Any golfer who wants to shoot lower scores should get fit for driver, for irons (including hybrids), for wedges, and for putter.

When I decided to take my own advice on this and make sure my clubs were right for my swing, size and stance, I went to the PING plant in Phoenix and had a professional fitting done. Other manufacturers offer something similar, but

PING is in my area and there is a lot about the company and their equipment I like, so it was easy—and free.

Since then I've learned a lot more about club fitting, and I know you could go online and figure out a lot of it yourself, but since you're already here, allow me to share some things that will be useful for you to know and help you with your game.

Irons

There are three parts to an iron: the club head, the grip, and the shaft that both of those are attached to. (Usually there is a ferrule—that little piece of plastic at the end of the shaft. It is purely decorative and weighs nothing, so I'm not counting it.) None of those components are made solely of iron, of course, but many years ago the heads were iron and the name has stuck.

The job of the grip is to help you hold the club lightly and firmly at the same time while giving you a good "feel" for the club. Its other job is to look cool and dress up your clubs.

The job of the head is to hit the ball up into the air and control its flight. Please note that hitting the ball up into the air is not your job, it is the job of the club head, and it is much better at that job than you are.

The final component, the shaft, provides distance between you and the ball (length) and allows you to swing the head so that it contacts the ball at the proper angle at the right time.

So far it sounds pretty simple, but if you take those three components and add them together, you will find that there are as many as twelve different areas to be considered when finding the right club for you.

In the shaft alone you should consider the length (longer shafts can increase club head speed but also increase launch angle and generally increase flexibility), the material (steel shafts have less rotational force than graphite but weigh more and feel more harsh on off-center shots), the flexibility (there are no industry standards, so stiff from one company might be regular from another company), and the weight. And those are just the big pieces.

For most of us the only sensible answer is to do a custom fitting. The other option is to go to a course or golf shop that has a lot of demo clubs and try them all out to see where you get your best results. Or borrow clubs from your friends and try those to see if they work for you.

If you truly want to shoot lower scores, though, please do not ignore your irons and focus exclusively on your driver and putter. Whether your set is made up of traditional irons or includes several hybrids, you will need to rely on those clubs a lot during a round.

Almost every par three starts with an iron. Almost every hole-in-one is made with an iron. Almost every approach shot is an iron. Almost every kick-in birdie is set up by an iron. Still, they don't get much glory and we don't speak of them in glowing terms, and too many players neglect them on the driving range.

If irons were part of your body I suppose they'd be the internal organs. You want them to work but you don't show them off and you don't pay much attention to them. Change that (the attention part, I mean), keep them clean and in good working order. You'll be better for it

Driver? Love it

John Cook says he was told by Ken Venturi, "You have to fall in love with the driver." Venturi was mentored by Ben Hogan, and Hogan said the three most important clubs in the bag were the driver, the putter, and the wedge.

Not everyone agrees with that order of importance, with the legendary teacher Harvey Penick saying the three most important clubs are the putter, the wedge, and the driver.

Statistics would agree with Mr. Penick more than Mr. Hogan. In fact a study of top collegiate golfers for two seasons (1992-93 and 1993-94) revealed that driving accuracy was basically the least important factor in scoring, affecting scoring average by about 1.5%. The biggies were a combination of greens in regulation and putts per round, which together accounted for 93% of overall score.

Perhaps the most surprising finding in that study was that every five fairways missed only decreased greens in regulation by one. So if you hit twelve fairways and twelve greens in one round and only seven fairways in the next round, by those statistics you would hit eleven greens in regulation.

But you still have to fall in love with your driver.

Why? There are at least two factors that those statistics either did not or could not measure. The first is proximity to the hole, which can now be and is measured for Tour players. Hitting from the fairway is, as you would imagine, better.

Very early in the 2015 PGA Tour season the leader in proximity to the hole from the rough had an average of 30 feet 4 inches, and the last place player's average was almost 71 feet.

The leader in proximity from the fairway had an average distance of 26 feet 4 inches, which you might think of as only marginally better, but the last place average from the fairway was 46 feet 2 inches. In fact the 75th ranked player from the fairway hit the ball closer to the hole than the 10th ranked player from the rough.

The second factor, which I suppose still can't be measured, is confidence for the rest of the hole.

Most players I observe, including myself, feel better about themselves and about a hole if they start with a good drive. On days when I'm hitting my driver well the feeling seems to spill over into the rest of my game, and I tend to hit my irons and approaches better as well. Even if it is just one less thing to worry about, accurate driving is something you want to have in your bag.

But most of us don't choose a driver for accuracy. If we did we would add loft to our driver and shorten the shaft. Instead we consult the rule book to find out what the maximum length of a driver can be (48 inches) and wonder if we can get more roll if we go down to 9 degrees of loft instead of 10.5. We want distance, baby, distance!

I totally get that, so let me tell you the best way to add to your driving distance.

Hit the ball on the sweet spot.

Clubs today are very forgiving, especially driver heads, but proper ball/club contact is still the primary distance factor. Interestingly, if you learn to make great contact with the ball you are also likely to become more accurate.

I do agree with the folks who say to first learn how to hit the ball really far and then dial back your swing until you can hit it really straight. If you didn't learn that way, you can still add power to your driver game (and irons), but it will be a little more work.

Learn to love your driver, learn to hit it right where you want it to go, and work with your pro to see if you can find a few extra yards. All of that will help in some ways, and the thing that is likely to help you the most is getting it in play.

Don't just get the shaft, select one

There are driver shafts that retail for as much as $1,000, club head and grip not included. If you played professionally and that shaft could save you even one stroke every four days, you could easily afford it.

A stock shaft, even in a premium driver, costs the manufacturer less than $5. Does that mean a $1,000 shaft is 200 times better? Of course not, but it is better, and so is almost any expensive shaft better than those that come stock.

This is not to say that a stock shaft is terrible or won't work for you. But if you spend $300 or $400 on a driver, wouldn't you want to know that the shaft is the best one for your swing speed and launch angle? The only way to know that precisely is to go to a club fitter and try different shafts with different weights, different kick points, and different materials.

You might end up spending an extra $100 to $200 for a shaft that works just right for you, and while that is a real investment it is one that could pay dividends for a long time.

The same is probably true for your irons, and you should not neglect the task of finding shafts for those clubs that give you the proper height, the proper spin, and the proper distance.

Lighter weight shafts (steel or graphite) are often a good idea for irons as well as for drivers, and they always have this advantage: even if you don't hit the ball any farther, a lighter weight shaft will allow you to throw the club farther when you get mad. (Just kidding. Please don't throw your club.)

Look, your putter, and your wedges

If a golf club does not look good to you when you put it on the ground, even in a golf shop, do not buy it. That is true across the board. Golf is a game of confidence, as Dr. Bob Rotella noted in the title of one of his books, and if the clubs look "off" to you in any way your confidence will be hurt. You must believe in those clubs, every one of them. This is entirely subjective, of course, but it is critically important.

By the way, getting your putter fit is at least as important as getting your driver fit. You may hit your driver 14 times in a round, but you'll usually hit double that number of putts. Invest time and money in your putter, and make certain you have complete trust in it. No club in your bag, including your driver, has as much power to save you as your putter.

Wedges are also very important in scoring, so make sure you pay attention when buying your wedges. As I write, there are now two online-only companies that make excellent wedges. One of those will customize the clubs for you (including the grind of the sole and stamping on the blade) and give you 90 days to try them out, then take them back if they don't work for you!

The spin zone

One last word about wedges, and it has to do with spin. People often ask me how to hit a pitch shot from 30 or 40 yards that hits the green, bounces once or twice, then checks up quickly.

I explain the technique, which includes a lot of spin, and then I take a look at their wedge. More times than not I'll tell them that a Tour player would have a tough time making a ball spin with the club they are using because the grooves are so worn.

Professional golfers who like to spin their wedge shots do not play with worn grooves. For that matter they also use a ball that spins rather than a distance ball, and they play on greens that react to spin. Of course they know how to hit the shot, and I'll just say in that regard that spin is primarily the result of speed and angle of attack.

Worn grooves, especially on your wedges, are a factor you should pay attention to if you want to control the spin on your shots, even on short shots.

Have a ball

The final piece of playing equipment you need to settle on is the golf ball. It's pretty hard to buy a bad golf ball these days, but I think it is important to find a model you like and stick with it. Personally I use a premium ball—the kind that costs about $4 per ball. Some people think that is a lot to spend, but even if it is there are two ways to lower that cost dramatically.

First, there are online companies that will sell you used golf balls that are like new (and they really are) for half that price. Shipping costs may raise the per-ball cost to $2.50, but if you watch for sales you can get basically brand-new premium balls for just over $2 each.

Second, most premium balls go on sale once or twice a year if you are willing to buy three or four dozen.

Even when I pay full price, I think of it this way: I use a golf ball on average for 36 holes. Premium balls are more durable than cheaper balls, and I once used one 100 holes. Of course I've also used a ball for one shot, drowning it in the process. (If you buy used balls and find one with LG stamped on it in red, let me know.) Anyway, if I say the average cost for a round of golf is $35, I just add the cost of a ball to the round. So now it is $39. (Really $37, but I figure it at a ball a round.) If I buy a soft drink and a bag of peanuts from the beverage cart, I'm spending more than I spend on a golf ball and I'm using that up almost immediately. It's just part of the cost of playing the game. Want to cheap out? Drink water on the course and bring a peanut butter sandwich with you, but use a good golf ball.

Even "distance" balls these days are well made and consistent, but they are distance balls primarily because they spin less in the air and roll more on the ground. Sometimes you know those by brand name, and sometimes you can tell a difference in a ball because it is harder. How do you know it is harder? It feels harder, right? Not so much.

If you couldn't hear, you probably wouldn't be able to feel the difference between a Pinnacle (hard) and a Titleist Pro V1 (soft). In fact you can test this by taking different golf balls onto a green with a friend and hitting some putts.

Close your eyes (you can putt without looking, I know) and have your friend put down a ball for you to putt. You'll be able to "feel" the difference and identify the balls, even without looking.

Now put in earplugs and repeat the experiment, and you will not be able to identify which ball is which. Sound is a huge part of feel, from putter to driver and everything in between.

For several years I used a Titleist Pro V1, and I liked the feel (sound) of it and the way it behaved around the green. Then, through Links Players, I met and caddied in a qualifier for Isabelle Beisiegel, a former LPGA Tour player. She was using a Pro V1x, which is a "harder" ball.

When I asked her about that choice she reminded me that she lives in Oklahoma, where it is often windy on the course. She found that she could control the ball better in the wind with the V1x.

Being the impressionable fellow I am, I figured I'd give it a try. For me the question wasn't so much about wind, it was about being able to control the ball around the green, specifically with pitch shots and chip shots. It did spin a bit less, but I liked the "feel" of it and it worked well for me, so I stuck with it.

How the ball responds for you around the green is an important starting point for better players, because you should have confidence that the ball is going to behave a certain way when you chip it or pitch it.

Whether you are talking about Titleist or Callaway or TaylorMade or Bridgestone or Wilson or Nike or any other premium ball, you'll notice that there are some PGA Tour players who use the "softer" and some who use the "harder" ball. For them it is about control of the ball in all conditions, from chips to drives, from high, long irons to knock-down wedges.

Once a player gets used to a ball and how it reacts, as well as to how it feels (sounds), you'll find that it is almost as challenging to change that as it is to change his or her grip. That's even true for me. I recently found a brand new Pro V1 and thought I'd play it for old-time's sake. After two holes I gave it to my buddy, because it just didn't feel right. And he was just fine with that.

Feet, don't fail me now

Bill Walton, Hall of Fame basketball player, tells the story of "socks" at his first college practice at UCLA. The legendary coach there, John Wooden, gathered the team and told them their first lesson was how to put on their socks, and if they wanted to learn the right way to do that, they should take off their shoes and socks.

Walton and one of his teammates declined that offer and went off to the court, where they were soon joined by the rest of the team. Practice then began in earnest, including start-and-stop drills, quick-direction-change drills, and wind sprints.

The next day Walton and his pal who did not learn about putting on their socks had terrible blisters, while no one else on the team did.

As it happens, Bill Walton's professional career was shortened because of foot problems. But it wasn't blisters, because he had learned that lesson the hard way.

If you walk a golf course when you play, you might travel as many as seven miles on your feet. Even if you ride, you'll probably walk more than three miles. If your feet get tired, or your shoes don't fit well, or if they don't offer proper support for a golf swing, you are risking injury and certainly adding strokes to your score.

Yes, premium golf shoes can be expensive. But like premium golf balls, they will be better for your game and they will last longer.

And by the way, if you wear shoes that have "soft spikes," change those spikes at least once a season. Don't just replace the worn spikes, replace them all. It will add power to your stride, and maybe even your shots.

Other "equipment"

When you are considering equipment, include your glove (if you use one), your clothes and your hat. All of those should fit you properly, and if they don't they can easily add a stroke or more to your round.

This may sound strange, but I personally think it is important to feel good about how you look on the course. For me, that means I'm going to wear clothes designed for golf in both their cut, their fabric and their look. At least people will think I'm a player until I get to the first tee, and that's worth something.

part two: three easy pieces
Go long? Maybe. Go short? Definitely.

The second easiest thing you can do to lower your scores is to spend 75% of your practice time in the short game and putting areas and 25% on the range. I write that knowing that if I can get you to even 50/50 I will have made progress, and so will you.

The great majority of your strokes in any round, unless you are already shooting par or better, will take place from within 50 yards of the hole and in. You will hit your driver no more than fourteen or fifteen times in a round and you'll hit around 30 putts, and yet you probably hit more practice drives than you do practice putts.

I get it. You think you can putt but you don't think you can drive.

Years ago I had a small solo singing part in a church play, but a large speaking part. With little confidence in my singing, I practiced those few bars of music far more than I practiced all of my speaking combined.

When the cast came together for rehearsal I noticed that my friend, a terrific singer who had a lot of songs in the play, was nervously practicing his two or three speaking lines!

That is why so many of us spend time hitting drivers on the range. The real reason is not to become a great driver of the ball, it is to avoid embarrassment. Like I said, I get it.

Even if you can putt, or at least putt well enough to avoid embarrassment, you can be a better putter than you are now. Ben Crenshaw was one of the greatest putters on the PGA

Tour, and he practiced his putting even after he achieved that status. How much more do I need to practice putting? But, like you, I tend to work on the parts of the game where I'm less confident.

When I recognize that flaw, I force myself to spend time on the parts of my game I feel good about. That actually helps me feel good about myself, and the time I spend working on the other parts is therefore more productive.

People who spend hours practicing the swing but only minutes on the putting and chipping greens and practice bunker sometimes wonder why their scores don't improve. They are working hard; they are just not working on the right things. Go to any course when it is busy and the number of people in the short-game area will be far less than the number on the range. Unless of course you go to a tournament, because good players know where the saved strokes are to be found.

There is no need for me to emphasize this further, because you know I'm right. But something gets in our minds, and off to the range we go. Even if our scores don't come down, we do enjoy hitting a large bucket and then talking about how hard we are working on our game. Sigh!

Add to the beauty

There is another reason why many of us prefer to hit balls on the range rather than chip and putt and play in the sandbox, and that reason is beauty.

Several years ago I had a lunch meeting with tennis legend Sandy Mayer, and after the meeting we separately and independently decided to go to a nearby driving range. As I was looking for an empty bay I saw Sandy, and I walked over and said, "I just had lunch with a fellow who looks a lot like you."

During that brief conversation I asked the former Wimbledon doubles champion if he preferred hitting a great serve in tennis or a great drive in golf, and with little hesitation he chose golf.

"A great serve in tennis is fun, but it only lasts about two seconds. A great drive in golf lasts about eight seconds, and watching it rise and fly and fall is beautiful."

That was good insight, and we really are pleased by the beauty of a well struck golf shot. The farther it flies, the more we like it. The promise of that beauty has kept me on the range many times when I should have been on my way home. It also has kept me from the short-game area when that was where I belonged.

The answer to that is to add to the beauty of short game shots. They will never be as dramatic as a long drive, but they have a beauty all their own. It is seen in precision, in finesse, and in creativity, and it is felt in touch.

Personally I need to think about this aspect more. Too often I have a utilitarian approach to the short game, and that leads me to thinking about technique. That, of course, destroys the opportunity to enjoy the beauty.

It's like going to an art gallery to see a beautiful painting but focusing on the frame. Yes, the frame is an integral part of the piece and it has its own attractive qualities, but the greatest beauty is inside the frame. Learn to find beauty in chip shots, pitch shots, bunker shots, running shots, flop shots, and even in short putts, and your enjoyment of practicing the short game will increase markedly just as your scores will decrease. And that's beautiful

Here's a lesson: take a lesson

Early in my golf career I relied on my natural ability far too much. I also relied on my own ability to read a book about a golf swing, or watch a video, and apply those instructions with great success.

Mixed success would be far more accurate. The teachers are often terrific and have a great way with instructing, so I'm not blaming them. The problem is, they can't see what I'm doing right or wrong. And neither can I.

If you want to get better at making the ball go where you want it to go, whether that is with a driver or a putter, take a lesson in person from a professional teacher.

A few words of advice on working with a pro are in order here.

The first is that it is as much your responsibility to learn as it is the teacher's responsibility to teach. Show up early, eager, warmed up and focused. Know what you want to work on and say so, then listen carefully to what the pro has to say. If you do not understand some instruction, don't pretend that you do. Ask for an explanation or a different way of saying the same thing, along with a demonstration. Be an active learner and your pro will be better.

Second, your pro will first try to establish rapport with you and in that process may ask you about other sports you play or hobbies you have. Don't think you are being patronized, because those questions have a real purpose. They help find common ground between the professional and you and can help the pro use language you understand to explain some complex aspect of the game.

Third, I recommend finding a professional who will work with what you have rather than trying to remake your swing in his or her image. If the first fifteen minutes include a lot of "we need to change this" language, you may want to consider looking elsewhere. To me that sounds like a pro who is planning on sending his kid to college with your money.

Joy

The final easy thing you can do to lower your scores is to learn to enjoy the game of golf and truly have fun playing it. Be happy that you get to play, to be outside in this beautiful world on a beautiful piece of property hanging out with beautiful people. (Even if they aren't movie-star beautiful on the outside, I'll bet they're beautiful on the inside.)

Start with that attitude before you even get to the course, and it will serve you well once you are there. Believe it or not, this will also help you focus, which is a very big deal indeed when it comes to lowering your scores.

How? When you are happy you are less easily distracted and everything is a little bit less about you. Staying in the moment, which means you are not thinking about results or other future events but are truly present, is almost a prerequisite to focusing well on each shot. If you get to the course with a surly attitude and a negative mindset, it will be very difficult for you to be positive over a putt.

So to recap these "easy" secrets, get fitted, get to the short game area, get a lesson (if you need one), and get happy. Just doing these three or four things should reduce your Index, and even if they don't they will most certainly increase your enjoyment of the game.

* * *

PUTTING IT INTO PLAY

I often wonder why we ignore the easy stuff. Perhaps it is because golf is supposed to be hard, or because we mistakenly think that only through blood, sweat and tears do we deserve to improve.

No, that can't be it. If it were, then the whole "buy this driver that looks like a locomotive and you'll drive it for miles straight down the tracks" industry would dry up.

I think it must be that we simply don't think of the obvious stuff, like getting clubs that fit us and using one brand of golf ball long enough to understand what it does around the greens.

But both in golf and in life we ought to be looking for the things that are simplest to fix before we engage in some struggle that will be long and hard. Perhaps you remember a scene from one of the Indiana Jones movies, where Indy finds himself facing a monster of an evil man who has murder in his heart and a long sword in his hand. The atmosphere is tense and it looks for all the world like Mr. Jones is done for as the assassin comes rushing at him, sword raised to strike. Then Indy pulls out his pistol. Having the right equipment really can make a difference.

Not us. We want to fight that assassin called a slice, and

we'll spend hours watching YouTube videos trying to find the secret swing, when all the while we just had a driver with too little loft and a face with a fade bias.

Look for the easy stuff first, and then if you have to fight hand-to-hand on the range with the part of your game that is causing problems, at least you'll go into battle with the right equipment, the right plan, and the right attitude. And the solution could still be easy.

2

Before You Swing

For most of his career the great Jack Nicklaus was coached by a man named Jack Grout. Their relationship was long and solid, and Jack would go to Jack at the beginning of each season for a "refresher" before he went back out on Tour. He did this, as I understand it, even after he had won many majors.

The refresher wasn't about the latest swing theory or how Jack could get more distance. It was simply about the basics: grip, posture, alignment.

Tracy Hanson was a four time All-American golfer in college, a USGA Public Links champion, and played on the LPGA Tour for more than 15 years. While she claims not to be a teacher of golf, I've seen her conduct excellent clinics. All she talked about there, unless asked about something specific, were her basics: grip, posture, alignment and tempo. And people improved.

Years ago a friend who was the head professional at Medinah Country Club (Chicago) conducted a golf clinic at the athletic club where I was the general manager, and he told us then that 80% of failed golf shots are the result of something that was wrong before the swing even started. In other words, either the grip, posture, aim or alignment were flawed in the setup, and that is why the shot was missed.

Since then I've heard people say it might be as much as 90%, so clearly the number of shots missed because of a faulty setup is very high. Thinking about that, it seems to me that there is little excuse for most of the mistakes we make.

When we do miss a shot, what is the first thing we suspect as the problem? "It must be something in my swing," we say.

After all, how could we get just standing there wrong? But we do, because we don't pay attention to it and we can't really see it. We walk up to the ball, stand to one side of it, grab the club, look down the fairway or at the flag, get six or seven swing thoughts in our head (freezing in place for so long while we process all those thoughts that our fellow players suspect we have gone to sleep), and then we suddenly come back to life and lash out at the ball. Yikes!

Get a grip

When was the last time you really looked at your grip? Did you know your grip can wander over time and that it might not be where you think it is? A faulty grip can cause all kinds of issues in your shots, from banana-slices to duck-hooks, two terms I find amusing until I hit one of them.

Side note: Rather than disparaging fruit and fowl by associating them with bad golf shots, I now use political names and terms. In my parlance a shot that goes way left is a "Nancy Pelosi," while one that goes way right "would make the Tea Party proud." If you decide to use those yourself, I offer just one word of caution: the people you are playing with may be sensitive, and they are definitely carrying clubs.

And now, back to grip.

Arnold Palmer famously tells the story of his father, "Deacon" Palmer, placing Arnold's young hands on a club for the first time. He worked them into the proper position and then told his son, "Don't ever let go of that grip." Arnold to this day credits that as an important part of his success, and that makes sense to me.

Yes, there are fine players whose grips deviate from standard significantly. Just because it works for them does not mean inventing your own way of holding the club is ideal. Those players are the exception rather than the rule. So check your grip often, and don't let go.

Aim, ready, swing

"Ready, aim, fire" sounds a lot better than "aim, ready, swing," and it might even work in golf. But I don't recommend it. The "ready" part includes standing up to the ball, aligning your body, and settling your mind. All of those depend to some degree on aim. Aim depends on the intended shot along with the intended final destination for the ball, and all of that should happen before you align your body and settle your mind.

Your aim, at least for the initial flight of the ball, is basically where the palm of your trailing hand is pointed. Most of the time the club face mirrors that aim, but not always.

I was playing a club level tournament with my brother in Virginia when I tried a shortcut on a par 5 and drove into the trees on the left. This was no "Bubba shot" at the Masters, but I did have to hit about a thirty-yard hook and the ball needed to travel about 180 yards. Bill took a studied look at the situation and then said, "You can't hook it that much and hit it that far. Just punch it out." Which was tantamount to a challenge, even though he meant it as helpful.

I aimed the club face at the green, aimed my right hand thirty yards to the right of the green, said something clever like, "Oh yeah?" and swung mightily at the ball. It started right, curved left, and came to rest in the back right fringe of the green. It's difficult to say who was more surprised, but he was more pleased, which pleased me to no end.

Take very good care of your aim. Practice it, work on it, and get it right. Once you have a good aim, hold on to it and let your alignment be guided by it rather than the other way around.

By the way, you can hit a fine golf shot with poor alignment, just as you can shoot a free-throw in basketball without facing the basket. You do it every time you walk up to a short put and tap it in without taking time to align your feet, which is probably several times per round.

Many golfers even putt and chip with a stance that is almost facing the hole, and that is fine. Aim trumps alignment, but good alignment will still serve you well.

Of course to have proper aim and alignment you must first

have selected a target, and it probably shouldn't be "somewhere down the fairway." Make it specific rather than general, make it small rather than large, and make it stick in your mind. Without choosing a target of your own, the course architect will choose one for you. Or didn't you know they did that?

The goals of the golf course architect are many, but one of the big ones is to attract your eye to trouble.

Stand up to the ball to hit it without picking out a target first, then turn to look down the fairway. What do you see? Trouble. The bunkers, the trees, the water hazard—all of those will stand out and your eyes and mind will be drawn to them. If your mind is focused on one of those, the likelihood that your ball will go there is greatly increased.

So get your sequence right. Acquire a target, aim, and then prepare your body and your mind to swing, propelling the ball to the target. It really is a simple game, at least when you say it like that.

Good posture is for more than just good looks

Posture includes things like ball position, knee flex, hip flex, and weight distribution. Because it isn't my purpose here to delve into "how" to hit a ball, I'll refrain from getting deeper into how to get physically ready to hit a ball. By this time you should know all of that and you probably do, but if you are like most of us you could pay more attention to it than you do.

I will recommend one thing regarding posture, though: learn balance.

A big part of the reason for good posture is to help you find and maintain proper balance, and balance is critical to any athletic endeavor. That includes being prepared to hit and then actually hitting a golf shot, whether that is a drive or a putt.

Some club fitters have simulators that include a balance board. That piece of equipment will calculate and display your balance electronically. When you begin with good balance a proper weight shift in and through the swing will be much easier to achieve.

If you don't have access to something like that, there are other ways to determine just where your balance is as you set up for a shot. The simplest, and one you always have with you, is feel. Your feet are very sensitive to slopes and weight, you just have to pay attention to them.

It's also a great idea to practice hitting full shots, especially wedges, with your feet close together. Your balance will improve as you do that, and consequently you'll be more aware of setting up to a shot and being off balance.

All of these happen before the swing ever begins. Unless you are playing a tournament or are holding up the group behind you, there really is no time limit for you to get these things right. Still, you should be able to get them right in just a few seconds if you have practiced them and know how to check them.

Tempo, tempo, tempo

Tempo, which is generally thought of as part of the swing—and it is—exists in more than just the swing, so allow me to get to the fringe of swing instruction and say a word about that.

The value of tempo in every shot you hit cannot be over-stated. That is true, to be redundant, from driver to fairway woods to hybrids to irons to bunker shots to pitch shots to chip shots to putts. Every swing, every putt, every chip, every trouble shot (especially every trouble shot!) should be executed with tempo. If a poor setup is the cause of 80% of failed shots, poor tempo is the cause of most of the rest.

There are books and videos about tempo, and you may want to investigate those because they could be useful to you, but here is a "secret" to tempo that I have not seen discussed in quite this way: your swing tempo begins before the setup.

If you happen to have a tape of Annika Sorenstam play-ing a round of golf, or if you can find a video of one of her rounds, put it on and get out your stopwatch. Hit "Start" when she begins walking toward the ball and hit "Stop" when her club strikes the ball. Do this on four or five different shots, and you will not find more than one second of differ-ence in any of them.

I pick Annika here because she is the poster child for consistent tempo, in my mind, but virtually every great player does this. So if you can't find a tape of Annika, record a tournament (men or women, though you'll learn more from the women) and pick a player you can time. Especially pick a player who is playing well (they'll be on screen the most if they are leading or contending) and check the consistency of the timing on their approach to the ball and ball strike.

Actually you can begin to set a tempo for the day in your mind by the music you listen to on the way to the course, or a tune you hum in your head as you are warming up, but with or without music, start your swing tempo in your approach to the ball, keep that tempo in your swing, and you will score better.

One addition: Aaron Baddeley is one of the finest putters in the game. If you get a chance to watch him live or on TV, time him on the green from approach to putt and you'll get the same kind of results you get with Annika. Consistent tempo in the setup leads to consistent tempo in the swing, which results in lower scores.

* * *

PUTTING IT INTO PLAY

The basics are called that for a reason, but just because we learned them a long time ago doesn't mean we are through learning about them or improving our use of them.

For many years I used an interlocking grip, and then a teaching pro convinced me that an overlap would work better for me. So I switched and I played just fine. I don't know that I was instantly (or even eventually) any better, though, so a couple of years ago I switched back to an interlock. Jack and Tiger are both interlocking grip guys, and they've done OK, so I don't figure it'll hurt me.

It turns out, though, that my right hand grip had recently turned to the right and I didn't even know it. One of my colleagues at Links Players, Jeffrey Cranford, who is both a teaching professional and an outstanding player, saw it in a glance.

So do what I should have done and what Jack Nicklaus

did, and find someone who has eyes to see and have them periodically check your setup. Feel is not real, so you are not likely to get this right by saying, "it feels good." You, or someone, has to look.

In all of life, taking care of the basics and having someone help make sure you do that well is a good idea. Tell your family you love them, even if you think they know it. Appreciate the wonders of the creation around you. (Stop and smell the roses, as Walter Hagen would say.) Sleep well, eat well, thank God for golf and for other blessings, and treat others as you would have them treat you.

Remember that being called a basic does not make something less important, it makes it more important. Practice your setup, practice your tempo. Always look to these first if there is a failed shot, and have them checked often. Your scores will improve.

3

Yes, You Still Have To Practice

A couple of years ago I said to my wife, "I'm playing the best golf I've played in more than thirty years."

To which she replied, "When was the last time you practiced and played as much as you are now?"

She already knew the answer and understood that there was a direct correlation between the amount of time I was practicing and playing and the quality of my game. I never lost the ability to hit some excellent shots or to shoot an occasional low score, but now I was back in the 60s and my Index was dropping steadily every month, all the way back to .4, with a plus-Index just around the corner.

Then I joined the staff of Links Players International—truly a marvelous blessing—and the time available to practice was once again reduced dramatically. The result was that my scores and Index began creeping up instead of down.

Because of my work with Links Players the last two years I have learned things about playing golf that I didn't know before, and some of those are in this book. All that should make me a better player, and it has. I shudder to think where my scores would be without that knowledge.

But even that has not been enough to balance out the lack of practice. In the same way, if you apply the ideas and information in this book to your game your scores will definitely go down. But if you combine those ideas with practice your scores will go down even more. So how can you make the most of the practice time you do have?

Make your practice count

The less time you have available to practice the more efficient you need to be. Of course efficiency is desirable in any practice session, but based on my years as a tennis pro and my own experience, I like the idea of training with some intensity, then taking a short break, then training with intensity, and so on. My mind seems to absorb more if I focus deeply and then let it rest.

A secondary benefit of this kind of practice is that it mirrors what happens during a round of golf. Even among professionals, very few golfers get on a course, get into a "bubble" of concentration and stay there. Almost everyone lets their mind relax between shots, so practicing with intensity and then relaxing, then getting back to intensity, is itself a good thing to practice.

By the way, the time you spend on the range or the putting green or chipping green before you go out to play a round of serious golf is not practice time. That is time to warm up, to prepare yourself mentally and physically (stretching), and to learn the speed of the greens. You may also get a feel for a swing or even establish a swing thought you will use that day. What you should not do is think of this as the time you practice.

A practice session is for the purpose of practicing various aspects of the game. A warm-up session is for the purpose of getting ready to go on the course and score. That is a big difference.

At the end of the next chapter you'll find a section on practice and attitude, so I won't go into that here.

What I will say here is that there are five areas you should be practicing in almost every session, and I'd put down even money that you aren't doing more than two of them currently and give you good odds that you aren't doing them all. Here they are, along with some thoughts on how to make them part of your practice.

Practice tempo

One day recently I drove to my golf club, which is about fifteen minutes from my house, with the intention of spending an hour working on my short game. As I pulled into the parking lot it suddenly struck me that my golf bag had not joined me on the trip. It was still in my garage.

I opened my trunk anyway, and as I stared at the empty space I reviewed my options. The decision was simple: I would borrow a putter from the pro shop and work on my putting.

The putter they let me borrow was not new and not for sale. (I wouldn't have trusted me either.) Its style was like mine, but it was an inch shorter than mine and a little bit lighter. Would it work? Certainly it would, I'd just have to modify my practice. I decided to focus on tempo, and I enjoyed the next 45 minutes as I did just that.

Even without my own putter that practice paid off. It helped ingrain a "one two" count on all of my putts, long or short, and the next time I putted in a round my tempo was terrific.

I bring up tempo in successive chapters because it is easy to forget to practice it. Even easier, I suppose, than forgetting your clubs. But try to remember them both.

Practice target

If you think back to your last round of golf (assuming you can remember these kinds of details, and most golfers can) and count the number of times on par four or par five holes that you had a target before you were on or close to the green, you would be the exception if you came up with two or three on any hole.

Most people who answer this question honestly say they had no real target off the tee (perhaps "the fairway") on 4s or 5s, no target on the second shot on a par 5, and finally acquired a target of the flag. You should have a target on every shot, and so should I, but I fail to do so for this simple reason: I don't practice target.

By this I don't mean that you should simply hit every shot at one of the flags or greens on the range, or even at the guy driving the range picker. Those are fine things to do, and you should do them, but there is more to it than that.

I mean that you should practice acquiring a target, and

you should not limit yourself to a flag. Flags on the range are natural targets, and we get that hitting at those is something like hitting at the flags on the course, but there are at least two problems with them.

The first is that flags are rare targets for tee shots on par 4s and 5s, and are also rare for a second shot on a par five, so learning to use them on the range won't help you on those shots, which add up to at least sixteen in a round, perhaps more.

The second is that there are quite a few times when hitting at the flag on your approach shot is a bad idea. If you get in the habit of only aiming at flags on the range, it will be hard to make yourself aim away from a flag on the course.

So what kinds of targets should you practice acquiring? The kind you'll use when you are trying to score.

Not long ago I had some range time and ran into a high-school player I know who was also working on his irons that day. I suggested we play a little game, and I did it because it incorporated three of the four elements we're considering here.

The game went like this: five shots each, alternating between players, at the chosen side of the green at any distance up to 165 yards. The player not hitting got to call either the shape or trajectory. Three points for hitting the proper side of the green with the called shot, two for hitting it with the wrong shape or trajectory, and one for any shot hitting the green on the wrong side. Most points out of five shots won the round.

Since I'm writing the book I'll say that I came out ahead after about thirty minutes of that competition, but the truth is we both won.

Half a green is a decent target, especially at 165 yards. If you are closer you might want to reduce the target size, or you might just like a smaller target, but the only important thing about a target is that you can truly acquire it.

If you have acquired it you can look away from it (perhaps back at your ball) and then back at the target without having to search for it. You have it in your mind's eye, so when you are ready to execute the shot your mind can see where it should help send the ball.

Practice finding all kinds of targets, not just flags, and have a target on every shot.

Practice creativity

In the game I mentioned above we forced each other to hit shots that curved one way or the other (or didn't curve), and we also forced shots of high, medium or low trajectory. We weren't being all that creative on our own, we were pushed into it.

When I was learning the game as a teenager, my friend and I would hit chip shots and pitch shots around our yard. There were trees of various shapes and heights, and we'd have to hit over them or under them or through some hole in the branches, and we loved it. We were learning creativity, although we didn't know it at the time, and it stood us in good stead when we played.

Perhaps the most well-known creative golfer who is active now is Phil Mickelson. He of the flop shot back over his head, or the shot off the pine straw at the Masters between two trees and over a creek to a front pin.

Those shots are related, because they both call on the

creative side, and Phil has practiced that since he was very young. It is not too late for you to start that yourself.

Of course Bubba Watson is also famously creative, and he even says that he far prefers to shape a shot than to try to hit one straight. That is marvelous stuff, and most of us would be better players with that kind of approach, but we'd have to practice it first.

The more you practice creativity, whether that means trying to hit a low fade or a high draw (both tough to pull off) or a stinger or an extra high shot or a seven iron that goes the distance of a wedge, the better you'll be when a shot on the course calls for some creativity.

Remember Tiger Woods' famous chip shot on 16 at The Masters that he purposely hit to the left of and past the hole, only to watch it slow down, reverse its course, and curve and roll all the way into the hole? That took imagination and creativity as well as skill. Do you think Tiger had ever practiced his creativity before that shot? Yeah, me too.

Practice pressure

I've met a few of the players who have competed in Golf Channel's reality show Big Break. All of them have said that the pressure there is greater than any other they have faced up to that point. They also said they came to like that experience, because it helped them believe that if they could take that pressure, they could take any pressure.

But for the most part, Big Break is not real golf.

It is real golf shots, and it does require real skill, but it isn't usually about getting the ball in the hole in the normal sense of golf. The good news about that is, you too can create pres-

sure for yourself in your practice sessions, and that is something you should do.

No, not every shot should be hit under pressure. Those creative shots you are practicing, for instance, should be free and
fun for the most part. Every shot should be hit with commitment, but that is different than hitting under pressure.

One way to create pressure when you are practicing alone
is to imagine, as many young golfers do, that this shot is for
the U.S. Open or this is for the club championship or this
is to get the girl (or the guy). No one knows better than you
what you want, so play for it.

A second way to practice pressure is to "punish" yourself
for a poor performance by making yourself repeat a process.
For instance I'll put four balls around a green and not leave
until I have chipped in from each of those four positions. Or
I'll have to hole out two bunker shots before I stop hitting
from the sand. Or I have to make 18 three-foot putts in a
row or start over from the beginning. Putts fourteen through
eighteen on that last drill are pressure packed indeed!

Personally I prefer "reward" pressure over "punishment"
pressure, so this is to win the Open appeals to me a little more
than having to start over when I miss a shot. The truth is, we
all miss shots and we will all always miss shots. I don't want to
fear failure; I want to embrace it as part of the game even as I
try to elude it.

Your own personality will be a guide to which kind of
personal practice pressure works best for you, but I'd like to
recommend that you start with the positive and minimize the
negative. "This is to win" seems to me a much healthier statement than "If I miss I'm a loser." You may lose if you miss,
but missing does not make you a loser.

Of course you can create all kinds of pressure when you are practicing with a partner, and some of those games are as much fun as being on a real course.

You don't have to hit every shot on the range under pressure, but you should practice pressure faithfully. After all, one day you might be on the first tee at The Masters. That is so much pressure that a pro once called it "the ultimate laxative."

Practice trust

Trust in golf is interesting. I described it like this to a friend: "You know that exercise where you fall backwards and you trust your colleague or teammate behind you to catch you before you hit the ground?"

He nodded yes.

"Trust in golf is like that except you have to fall *and* you have to run around behind yourself and catch you before you hit the ground."

No one has seen you mess up more than you have, so it is understandable if you have some trust issues with yourself. There is a pretty well known passage in the Bible where Paul writes, "I know I am rotten through and through so far as my old sinful nature is concerned. No matter which way I turn, I can't make myself do right. I want to, but I can't. When I want to do good, I don't. And when I try not to do wrong, I do it anyway" (Romans 7:18, 19 - New Living Translation).

Paul was referring to something far more important than golf, and as smart and wise as he was, he still could not trust himself to get it right. He needed divine assistance, as do we all.

Some days I think I need divine assistance on the golf

course, or at least I need some help in exercising trust. Other days I play as if I can do no wrong, because somehow I believe I can only do right. On those days if I miss a shot I don't think of it at all, dismissing it easily as an anomaly.

How can I do that more often? And, more importantly, how can you practice trust so it shows up in a big way on the course?

My recommendation is that you start with a shot that is fairly simple and has little risk, then move toward one that is fairly difficult and has more risk, trusting yourself along the way. Here is an example of one way I do that, but you can easily create your own.

I start with a pitch shot toward the range. I pick out a ball at some indeterminate distance (usually 30 to 40 yards away), then, using one of my wedges, I look at that ball, get my setup, and without further thought I take the shot and try to land within a couple of feet of the target. I do not measure the distance of the shot before hitting it. This isn't about precision, it's about trust.

Next I take about fifteen more shots like that using various clubs. Remember, my only real goal here is to build trust in my ability to judge the distance and hit a ball to that distance. If I happen to hit a great shot, all the better. There is no risk and potentially strong reward.

Then I move to my irons and I shape shots without consciously resolving how I will do that. In fact I hit the nine shots that the legendary Ben Hogan hit at the end of his practice sessions, and I do it with trust. (The nine shots are draw, straight and fade with low, normal and high trajectory.)

Do I always hit every shot perfectly? Of course not. Sometimes I have to convince myself that the ball faded, or that the trajectory was normal rather than high, but there is one thought I invariably come away with: I'm much better at those shots when I simply trust myself to hit them than when I consciously try to manipulate the ball in some way.

I have learned over the years how to hit fades and draws at different trajectories or this wouldn't work, but one of the keys to the whole "trust" issue is that I don't think I have to re-learn how to curve the ball.

One of the biggest barriers to trusting yourself on the course is to say, even subconsciously, "Here's how you hit that shot." In another context, imagine you are driving down the road and your front seat passenger is constantly reminding you how to drive.

"Look to the right and then to the left before you pull out into the intersection."

"That light is going to turn yellow so you'd better slow down."

"Make sure you turn on your blinker when you change lanes."

Does all that help your driving? No, it creates tension, distracts your natural focus, and in fact might make you a more dangerous driver.

That passenger is the same one who says, "To hit a fade off this tee you'll have to change your stance and swing along that line, but be sure to open your club face a little and...."

Does all that help your driving? No, it creates tension, distracts your natural focus, and in fact might make you a more dangerous driver.

Here's the deal. If you haven't practiced hitting a particular shot it will be difficult, if not impossible, to trust yourself to hit it for score, so don't try it unless it is an absolute must.

Hit a shot you can trust, then go back to the range and work on the new shot until you can trust it just as well, even if that takes days. Your arsenal and your confidence will both grow as a result.

Here's a story about one of those "absolute musts." Webb Simpson had a one stroke lead and a terrible lie next to the green on the 72nd hole of the 2012 U.S. Open. His caddie, Paul Tesori, described it as one he wouldn't have given him on a bet. The ball was on hardpan, but right behind it was 4-inch tall rough. This was at Olympic in San Francisco, and the 18th green is notoriously fast and sloped back to front, with the pin that day near the front.

Web first thought of hitting it 8 to 10 feet above the hole, assuring a two-putt and a playoff. If he chipped it at the hole and missed it at all, he could easily roll off the front of the green and down the slope as much as 30 or 40 yards, making even a bogey unlikely.

But there was a shot he had practiced a few times that had him use his wrists to kind of pop the ball out. He decided to try it. As Paul Tesori later told the story to an audience in Phoenix he said, "Thank goodness for talent." Web trusted himself and chipped it to about 3 feet, then made the putt to win the U.S. Open.

Practice trust on the range, then practice trust in practice rounds, then practice trust in escalating levels of competition. And when you hit a shot, ask your passenger to be quiet over there and trust yourself. You'll like the feeling.

* * *

Acquiring a target, being creative, having a good tempo, performing under pressure, and trusting yourself are all skills you will need on a golf course. I happen to believe they are also skills you will need in life. There we might call a target a goal, but the rest of the words can apply just fine.

Think of the places where you already apply those. When you are driving a car you have a destination in mind. If you run into a road block (construction, for instance), you may need to be creative in determining how best to get there. If there is a lot of traffic, or if you have to get there very quickly, you have to summon all your skills and perform under pressure. And all the while you have to trust your years of experience to steer the car, brake the car, accelerate the car, and keep the car and its passengers safe.

You could easily imagine a similar analogy for your work, I'm sure, or for raising a family, or for marriage. The great advantage that golf has over life is that you get to practice it. Practice these elements, and your golf and your life will improve.

4

Every Shot Really Does Count

It may be apocryphal, but I once heard it said that Bobby Nichols, winner of the PGA Championship in 1964 (he won by three over Arnold Palmer and Jack Nicklaus), was asked what the best lesson he'd ever received was. Without hesitation he said the lesson had come from his father, and it was this: Five is better than six, six is better than seven, seven is better than eight.

And if you asked Kevin Na about that, he might add that 16 is better than 17.

Na, an accomplished professional golfer, was one under par through the first eight holes of the 2012 Valero Texas Open, not far from the lead. Teeing off on the par-4 9th he appeared to have his game under control, but he pushed his drive right and into the trees.

These were not widely separated pines like you might see at Augusta National, they were dense hardwoods with a lot of branches, both new and old. It was as thick as a New York City sidewalk at rush hour, and Na had to climb over and through the undergrowth and fallen branches to even get to his ball. Once there, he had no swing at all and had to declare an unplayable lie.

While the rules allow for a drop, his only viable option was to take a one-stroke penalty and return to the spot from which he last hit, which was the tee.

Now hitting his third shot off the tee, Na pushed it right again into almost the same place as his first drive. And it got worse from there.

Ultimately Na escaped the woods, got to the green, and had a long putt for a score that some thought was a 13 and some thought was a 14. He tried to make the putt, but he missed. He did make the next one, though, for what turned out to be a 16.

Na is not alone in making a double digit score. John Daly (remember what we said in the introduction about length?) had an 18 on the par-5 6th hole at Bay Hill in 1998, which is the "scoring record" on a single hole on the PGA Tour since 1983. He did it by repeatedly (and unsuccessfully) trying to fly his drive 320 yards over water to a C-shaped green. *Tin Cup* in real life.

The host at that Bay Hill Invitational was Arnold Palmer, who himself once made a 12 in tournament play on a par-5. That was at the Los Angeles Open in 1961, and when reporters asked Palmer how he made 12, he famously answered, "I missed my putt for 11."

That answer points out something else Na and Daly and Palmer have in common, along with many other double-digit pros: they kept trying to get the ball in the hole.

That, of course, is the lesson Bobby Nichols' father was teaching him. Keep trying to get the ball in the hole, because even if it is your seventh stroke, that is better than taking an eight.

How many times have you had a putt for a double-bogey and not tried to make it? I remember vividly one time when it happened to me. I pushed my drive right on the opening hole par-5 into a hazard, dropped, hit an average shot across the fairway into the left rough, foozled my fourth shot into a green-side bunker, left it in the bunker, blasted my sixth out to about 12 feet past the hole, and, in a hurry to end the bleeding and get out of everyone's way, stabbed at the down-hill-right-to-left putt while saying, "Stick a fork in me and you'll see I'm done." The putt didn't go in, though it did stop inches from the hole and someone knocked it back to me.

In my mind I had recorded a 7 because under Equitable Stroke Control (ESC), a double-bogey is the most I can turn in on any one hole. But as we walked off the green my friend said, "Eight is a pretty nice start for a 1 handicapper."

Then it hit me that I had not made a double-bogey, I had made a triple-bogey. Why? Because I forgot that every shot counts. There is no ESC in tournaments, and there was no ESC in the game being played that day. No one there cared what score I turned in for handicap purposes, they cared about how many strokes I actually had on each hole.

Remembering that from the first tee shot to the last putt is one thing that consistently separates those who shoot low scores from those who don't.

This will be important to you if you are trying to get to or anywhere near scratch, but it is crucial if you are playing for a living. Here's why.

At the end of the 2014 PGA Tour season the top 125 in money earnings kept their job for the next year. The difference in money earned between Nicholas Thompson, who was 125, and Charlie Beljan, who was 126, was only $725. Without delving deeply into the stats it is hard to know what Charlie would have had to do to earn $726 more that year, but it could easily come down to one stroke in one of the 26 events he played in.

Now I don't mean to suggest that Charlie let up on a shot, but you can see how devastating letting your mind wander could potentially be.

How do you learn to play as if every shot counts? There are both physical and mental training methods to help. The good news is, you can learn to do it. The bad news? You have to work at it.

On the physical side, carry a blank piece of paper and a pencil. A scorecard will do, and so will a fine-point Sharpie, but you need to have immediate access to both, so they need to be in your pocket. It doesn't work to put them on a power-cart, or even on the tray of a push-cart.

Every time you take a stroke, whether actual or penalty, pull the paper and pencil out of your pocket and make a mark. Do this immediately after the stroke, even if it is a putt from twenty feet that stops one foot from the hole. When you make the one-footer, make another mark.

This forces you to recognize in real time that every swing, whether it is a long drive or a short putt, counts equally.

You can use the old four-ticks-and-a-slash if you like, but I don't recommend it. This isn't about keeping score, it is about understanding the equal weight of every stroke, so I like the idea of simply making a mark. If your paper ends up with ninety-nine marks, no problem. If it ends up with sixty-nine, that's fine. But every one of those marks counts the same.

Stopping in the moment to make the mark adds to the

idea of equality. My intent is not for you to hold up your group, and you need to be careful about that, so you may want to do this the first time when you are playing by yourself or with friends in a practice or social round. Try it for even nine holes, and you'll begin to see that every shot counts.

If you don't think you need a physical reminder and are strong willed enough, here is a way to accomplish the same thing just using your mind.

Before you hit any shot—even a tap-in—tell yourself that the shot you are about to hit is the only shot you are going to get to hit that day.

That will make each shot the most important shot you have, and you will focus much more sharply than if you had treated it like a throwaway.

This sounds much easier to do than it actually is, but if you savor each shot and enjoy each shot as if it were your only shot, you'll be amazed at how much more care you take with every drive and every putt.

This advice is fairly simple and yet rarely exercised: to score better you must remember that every shot counts equally— even the penalty strokes—and remember to take equally good care of each shot. The shots you take care of will take care of you.

* * *

PUTTING IT INTO PLAY

We're talking about golf here, but I'm sure you can apply this principle to other parts of your life. Every day counts, you might think, or every word counts or every opportunity counts. The truth is that we waste days and words and opportunities in much the same way we waste golf shots, and perhaps even for the same reason: poor practice.

When you practice golf, whether that is putting, short game or long game, you should practice more than just mechanics. What do I mean by that?

It's as simple as what the old football coach told his teams, "Practice like you want to play, because you'll play like you practice." Practice does not make perfect, practice makes permanent.

What I see on the range is men and women trying to make perfect swings. That is admirable but impossible, and I'll get into that more later. What I also see is men and women, but especially boys and girls—especially boys—failing to treat each shot with care.

Get in the habit of letting your mind wander on every third or fourth shot on the practice range, and you'll do the same thing on the course. Get in the habit of treating each shot on the range or short-game area or putting green like it is important, and you'll do the same thing on the course.

In life we have to have times that are work (productive activities for which we are paid), times that are play (non-productive and unpaid but entertaining), and times that are leisure (productive but unpaid activities, like reading a book or serving your church or community).

A balance between those three is important for us as humans, and we should never allow work (for instance) to dominate so much that we forget how to play or how to contribute without being paid.

Golf practice (and even playing) is much the same way. When I was playing my very best golf I practiced for several hours a day as well as playing at least 18 holes. I probably averaged about 300 balls on days I played (most days) and twice that many on days I didn't play. And of course I spent at least half of my practice time putting and on other short game skills.

I'm not going to tell you that I hit every one of those balls with care. Some of them were hit with focus, some were "play" shots, goofy things I'd never use on the course, and some of them were shots I wanted to learn but thought I'd rarely use (work, play, leisure).

What I didn't do as well as I should have was always try. I'd swipe at the ball and call it a joke if it didn't come off like I wanted. I'd aim at a target, stand over the ball, think my aim was wrong, and hit it anyway. I'd be thinking about something completely different than the task at hand and I'd still swing.

Why should I be upset with myself now when I do that on the course?

So practice like you want to play, because you'll play like you practice.

And by the way, even when you play golf, some days should be "play" golf—just have fun and don't even keep score; some days should be "leisure" golf—what you might call a practice round, where you work on things; and many days should be "work" golf, where you really try to score the best you can.

Incorporate the secret of trying to make every shot count into your practice, and you'll soon find that "work" golf is a lot closer to "play" than you ever thought it could be.

5

One Bad Shot Does Not Deserve Another

A friend of mine who owns property across the street from a golf course—and when I say street I mean a four-lane road with a sidewalk on each side of it and a speed limit of 45—told me that he collects quite a few balls each season, many more than he expected when he bought the place. But what he found interesting and did not expect was that he often found golf balls in pairs.

When I asked what he meant, he explained that he'd find a Pinnacle and a few feet away he'd find another Pinnacle. Or maybe it was a pair of Titleists or a pair of Nikes, and they often had the same look and even the same number. He could only surmise from the evidence that someone had hit a shot over the green and across the street (obviously out of bounds), dropped another ball, and repeated the shot. A repeatable swing is desirable in golf, but not in that scenario.

I wish I fully understood the mental phenomenon—and this is primarily a mental issue—that causes us to be seemingly unable to stop the bleeding. Something about neurotransmitters I'm sure, but whatever the cause, it is messy and painful.

The worst one I ever witnessed in person was in a high school sectional tournament. Our group came up on a par-four and there were already two groups on the tee. I asked a player from the group in front of us what the holdup was, and he pointed to the player on the tee. "He's already hit two balls out of bounds on the right, and he's about to hit again."

Part of the reason this was taking so much time is that the out-of-bounds on the right was not visible from the tee because of a line of trees. There was a marshal, however, located in a spot where he could see the flight of the ball, its eventual resting place, and the slope leading to property off the course. Once he confirmed that the ball was out of play, he emerged from the tree line and signaled back to the tee, giving either a "safe" sign or an "out" sign—a kind of active waving toward the out-of-bounds— which indicated that the player should hit again.

About that time the poor fellow on the tee did indeed hit again and I watched the drama continue to unfold. The ball started down the right side, began to turn more to the right, and disappeared over a little hill and into the tree line. Soon the marshal appeared and signaled, in a rather animated manner, that the ball was out of play. That was number three.

Eventually the golfer hit his fifth attempt into play. By that time it had become a battle between him and the marshal, at least in his mind, and when that last shot stayed in bounds the player gave his own signal (a lone, raised finger) back to the marshal. All of us on the tee laughed and then applauded.

And a few of us hit something other than a driver off that tee.

Over the years I've seen mini-versions of that scenario, and it always feels to me like a scratch in a record or a skip in a DVD. It gives me chills just to write about it. So how do you avoid it?

Bad shots happen, even to the very best players in the world. But it is rare for those players, or even for single-digit handicappers, to have those bad shots cost them more than the price of that one bad shot.

What is the secret to following a bad shot with a good one? I have a method I call ERR, as in Alexander Pope's "To err is human; to forgive, divine." I have just been human, after all, so I admit that I have erred and I avoid another error with this little system: evaluation, recalculation, resurrection.

Evaluate what just happened

Evaluation is simply a dispassionate assessment of the shot you just hit. It is about the shot and not about you as a person. Unfortunately I often see a different "E," and that is emotion. An emotional response to a good shot is just fine, but here we are talking about bad shots, and emotion should not be invited to the party.

Have you ever seen a player in your group hit a terrible shot under pressure and have his first response be one of self-derision? "You idiot!" is a phrase I've heard players use on themselves, even from my own lips. I've also heard various forms of swearing and seen clubs slammed on the ground, along with other kinds of emotional responses.

All of this judgment and display of emotion is understandable but not helpful. Rather than having a calming effect it has an adrenaline-inducing and mind-cluttering deleterious effect. Yes, the player has successfully communicated to everyone around that he has just hit a poor shot, although everyone around already knew that.

If you want to score better, you need to learn not to allow a bad shot to cause negative emotion. The response you want to a poor shot is much more rational, and an easy way to make your response rational is to simply evaluate what happened. If you were a TV announcer watching your shot from outside, what would you say? It would be something rational, like, "Well, folks, it looks to me like he lined up a little too far left and intended to hit a fade, but it didn't work. That ball is out of play, but he did hit it solid." As a TV announcer you would not say, "What an idiot!"

The best place to practice using evaluation rather than succumbing to emotion on poor shots is the driving range, and one of the best ways to practice it is to go to the range with your announcer-self along. Bring the "color" commentator, too.

If you've paid attention to the commentators when you've watched a tournament on television, you'll know that there is a professional announcer paired with a "color" analyst who is usually a retired (or semi-retired) professional golfer. The first of these analysts, and the man who set the tone for it all, was Byron Nelson, but the quintessential team in my mind was Pat Summerall and Ken Venturi.

The announcer's job is to simply tell the audience what is going on. The job of the color commentator is to add not only expert analysis to the mix, but some emotion (color) as well. When I ask my friends who watch golf on TV who they like to listen to, they rarely name the announcer. Why? Because we all naturally remember emotional comments and tend not to remember factual comments.

Earlier I mentioned the chip shot Tiger Woods hit on 16 at The Masters that went above and past the hole, hoping that it would roll down the slope and get close. It did that and then it trickled closer and closer and just as it looked like it was going to stop on the edge of the hole (you could clearly see the logo on the ball), the last bit of gravity pulled the ball down and into the cup.

If you saw that, you probably remember Vern Lundquist exclaiming, "In your life, have you ever seen anything like that?" I'll bet you can even do a pretty good impression of that very emotional line, which is probably in the commentators hall of fame today.

Lundquist was working the 16th tower, and in that role he mostly had to play the part of announcer but also had to be part-time color man. This was that side of him at its best, and we all felt the emotion he was feeling, which was a lot of fun and actually helps us remember Tiger's shot. But that was a good shot, not a bad one.

I'll say it again: emotion helps you remember things, including golf shots, but a rational comment does not add to the memory of most things, including golf shots. If you want to remember a shot and be able to repeat it more easily the next time, slather it with emotion. If you want to simply forget it, respond to it with logic and a rational comment.

So there you are at the range hitting shots, but your purpose is to learn to control your negative emotions so that you don't follow a poor shot with another poor shot. Your announcer and your color commentator are with you, watching. You are playing a game of some kind against yourself. The plan is to put yourself under pressure, which brings emotions closer to the surface.

Ready? Every time you hit a shot that is less than you expected, let the announcer talk about it in a matter-of-fact way. Since announcers always try to be accurate and usually kind, have your announcer say something factual but nice. For instance, "That was solid." Or, "That was on the right line."

By talking about your shots this way you are using evaluation rather than emotion, which is a much healthier approach for less than perfect shots.

Remember, on shots you don't like on the course only the announcer is allowed to speak. The turn of the color commentator will come later.

Evaluation on the course might include a look at why the ball went astray as well as a description of what the shot looked like.

When I evaluate I first go behind where the ball was played from and make sure my line was correct. I glance at the target I had and make sure I acquired it properly. Based on the shape of the shot and swing issues I know I fight, I'll sometimes evaluate those in context to see if they are culprits. In short it is fine to know why you missed—just don't be emotional about it.

Recalculate the variables

There is a natural tendency during recalculation to continue evaluation, and if it helps you that may be fine. Ideally, though, you will let that shot go completely out of your mind and recalculate as if this were (because it really is) a brand new shot. So I try, not always successfully, to compartmentalize each of these three steps.

The next step in not following one bad shot with another is recalculation. In other words, start over from the beginning. If you are still on the tee after hitting a ball out of bounds, put your club back in the bag and pretend you just got there. That means you'll have to gauge the wind, pick a target, and do all the things you normally do in your pre-shot routine. Perhaps you missed a calculation in your previous shot, or perhaps not, but this is a whole new shot, so recalculate.

Some thoughts about pre-shot routine are in order here, since calculation is an important part of that ritual. Almost every golfer who has been playing for any length of time has actions she goes through before every shot. She may not think of that as a pre-shot routine, but it is.

Since it is apparently natural for us to find a pattern of behavior that precedes a golf shot, why not make that purposeful and valuable rather than simply mechanical?

When you get into your car to drive, you have a "pre-shot" routine. You adjust the seat and get comfortable, you adjust the mirrors, and you put on your seat belt. You start the engine, you put your foot on the brake, you look around you and you look specifically in the direction you want to go, you put the car in gear, and you drive.

A pre-shot routine is very much like that. And since we're talking about driving, let's go through a pre-shot routine for hitting a drive.

You take your driver out of the bag and remove the head cover. You put it someplace, and ideally it is a similar place every time. You walk up to the tee and survey the hole, determining where you want your drive to finish and how you want to get it there. Based on that, you tee up the ball on the appropriate side of the tee box. You then stand behind the ball, confirming your choice of direction and shot shape. You acquire a target. You visualize the shot. You (perhaps) make a rehearsal swing. You step up to the ball (the "pre-shot" part is over, and the "shot" part now begins) and take your stance with the proper grip, posture, aim and alignment. You look back at your target while waggling the club in your hands to stay loose. You look back at the ball and the swing begins.

Did you notice the calculation part of that routine and where it occurred? That's right, it all happens before you even put your tee in the ground! You don't get that option for the rest of the hole, so take advantage of it when you can.

Always calculate the shot, and be finished with your calculations, before you step up to the ball. A proper pre-shot routine separates calculation from execution because calculation happens pre-shot and execution is the shot.

We'll revisit pre-shot routine in Chapter 13, Playing With KASH, but for now please make sure yours includes that time for calculation.

Resurrect your shot

The final step is resurrection, and this part is largely internal. We use the term "dead" in both positive and negative ways in golf. If you lay a putt dead, that is good because it is right next to the hole. If you hit a drive that stops rolling dead behind a tree, that is bad. When you hit a shot right at the hole and someone says, "That is dead on line," be happy. When you hit one over the fence and your friend says, "You're dead," evaluate.

Your friend is right, but only temporarily. You get to hit again, so you have new life, you have resurrection—you just have to embrace it in real time.

Clearly this is challenging, but the grieving process for the shot that went out must be quickly replaced with the joy of the new shot that lies before you. Understand that you are alive again and behave like it.

Remember, evaluation, recalculation, resurrection. Follow that process, and the likelihood of following one bad shot with another is greatly reduced.

* * *

PUTTING IT INTO PLAY

Each of the steps in ERR are powerful, even when used separately.

You might evaluate a shot that you would rate as a B but is still in play. You might recalculate even before you hit a shot by simply stepping away and taking another look, and you could employ resurrect during your round if you find yourself getting down mentally by saying to yourself, "Snap out of it!

This is a new hole and a new chance to score."

In fact, the better you get at using these tools individually the better you will become at using them together, but it is not an easy skill to assimilate.

The key to putting it all together, I believe, is to be dispassionate at the beginning of the process and increasingly passionate as you go through it. In other words, your evaluation (the announcer) must be cool and clinical while your resurrection should be a little more emotional. The recalculation, in the middle, should be logical but can also lean toward a positive thought like, "OK, this time I've got it."

You'll know you have this down cold when you hit a ball out of bounds and are not only not angry but are eager for your "new life" to begin.

I sometimes call this the Lazarus effect, remembering that Lazarus was resurrected after having died. Remember though, that Jesus said, "Lazarus, come forth." If he had just said, "Come forth" all the dead people in those graves would have been resurrected. Don't resurrect any shots you don't want to give another life to, let those shots stay right where they are.

You will also have noticed that I spent a lot more time on dispassionate evaluation than I did on recalculation and resurrection. That is because controlling your emotions for many of you will be the biggest stroke saver you can imagine. Get that one thing right, and much of the rest of this book will be far easier for you. Including the next chapter.

6

Don't Know Your Score Before You Shoot It

A few years ago I played golf in a regular Friday morning group. There were anywhere from six to sixteen of us on any given Friday, and we divided up after we arrived based on important factors like who had to be done early and who wanted to play from the back tees. Rarely, if ever, were the pairings made based on playing ability or scoring average. Two of our fellows, decades-long friends, often played together so they could wager their customary 10¢ nassau, but anyone could end up with anyone.

Many of us were either pastors or volunteer leaders in our various churches, and we played on Friday because it was the day off for most of us who were still working, and we played together because we loved each other's company—and for the most part we loved each other. No one played in this group for a chance to win money, the 10¢ nassau excepted.

One of our regular guys, Chuck, was someone I was paired with often. He could hit some great shots, had a solid short game, and knew the course well. Like most of us he wanted more length off the tee, but he did just fine.

One day I was paired with him when he shot an 80. I knew that because he was upset that he had bogeyed two of the last three holes and said that if he had just made one bogey he would have broken 80 for the first time.

"What?" I asked with genuine surprise, "You've never broken 80?"

He said he had not, and I said I couldn't believe that because he was quite a fine player. He insisted, and I said, "You play a round with me, just the two of us, and I guarantee that you'll break 80."

I didn't have to ask him twice, and a date was soon selected and a tee time booked.

As we pushed our three-wheeled carts to the first tee for the appointed round I explained the rules for the day. Chuck was not allowed to keep score—I would take care of that. And I was going to play, but I also might pick up at any time so I could focus on him. Further, I would have him tell me before each shot just what he had in mind and why, and if I saw alternatives I might ask him why he didn't choose one of those (like going under a tree instead of over it) or why he had chosen the path he had.

When the round was over Chuck had taken 78 strokes, and he was a happy man. I moved away shortly after that, but he wrote to tell me that he had followed that with a 79. He has in fact broken 80 on several occasions since that first day.

The truth is that most of us tend to think of ourselves as shooters of some small range of scores.

"I'm a nineties shooter."

"I shoot between 75 and 80."

"I'm in the mid-eighties."

With statements like that, we become prophets and our scores become self-fulfilling prophecies. Here is how it works, and how it can work for you and against you.

William James, the father of American psychology, wrote, "There is nothing so absurd but if you repeat it often enough people will believe it."

In other words, if you say it over and over and over it ultimately becomes truth for your audience—almost always including you. That's why the self-help mantra "Every day in every way I am getting better and better" actually works for many people, at least in the short term. It's also why telling a child repeatedly that he or she is or will grow up to be a failure can be so damaging.

If you tell yourself that you can't break 80, you are pretty much guaranteeing yourself that you can't break 80. If, on the other hand, you tell yourself that you are a 70s shooter, and if you come to believe it, that one statement alone will help you break through.

This assumes, of course, that you have the tools to accomplish what you are telling yourself you can do. If you have never flown an airplane it would be unwise to tell yourself you could fly one and then attempt to do so.

Fortunately the human mind, while it can be bent to believe something, will one day want proof of some kind.

Without that it will begin to think of the self-talk as deceptive and will guard against it in the future. So don't call yourself a long-drive champion unless you have the skills, and don't call yourself a consistent 70s shooter if that is thirty strokes better than your very best. But do talk to yourself in positive terms about your scoring ability.

Of course it is tremendously beneficial if someone else tells you that first, someone like a teaching professional or a player whose game you admire. But you can do this on your own, and your belief coupled with solid work on your game will get you there.

The place where I see this played out in the most insidious way on the golf course is by someone who is, like Chuck was, trying to break 80 for the first time. Such players have a tendency to know their score after the first nine. To break 80 on a par 72 course, a player has to shoot no more than seven over for eighteen holes, so if that player knows after nine holes that he is only three over, he knows all he has to do on the back is play basically the same. He even has one shot to spare.

But the I-can't-break-80 self-fulfilling-prophecy leaps in, grabs hold of his mind, and suddenly he is four over on the back with three holes left to play. The odds of his playing those three holes in par or less would warm the heart of a Las Vegas bookie.

If you know your score before you shoot it, your odds of playing better than that are very long. Two things will help you overcome your own belief system. First, resist the temptation to prophesy a "normal" score and instead prophesy for yourself a great score.

"Today is the day I shoot 78," you say. (Don't say 79, give

yourself some margin.) Say it often enough and you will begin to believe it, and then the odds are that you'll do it.

The second thing is to not keep score while you play. Either let someone else keep score while swearing on Calamity Jane that they will not tell you your score until the round is complete, or simply go back and add up your score when the round is finished.

Both of those include the distinct advantage of allowing you to focus on each shot as if it is a separate thing, and there is more later about how helpful that is for your game. Not knowing your score also keeps you from sabotaging a good round by pressing too much or by playing too defensively.

As a teenager I had some rounds under 70, one of them a 64, but they were on a short par-71 course that consisted of nine holes which were repeated from different tees on the back. Both the lack of length and the second look at the greens made it easier to score there than at some other courses, but I still shot in the 60s.

A few years later I found myself playing a par 72 course on an almost daily basis that was much more challenging, and I pushed and pushed to break 70. As I recall it I shot 70 on the number several times, and one of the things that held me back was knowing what I had to do coming in to get that elusive 69. If I needed par on the last, I'd make a bogey. If I needed a birdie, I wouldn't make the putt.

Then one day I resisted knowing my score until I could stand it no longer, which was in the middle of the fairway on the 18th hole. When I added it all up, I was four-under. Relaxed, I made the most routine par you can imagine for a 68. From that point on I was "a sixties shooter," and I broke

70 routinely.

As I noted above, it is not just about what you believe you can do or should do or will do, it is that belief is a much larger part of the picture than most golfers recognize. In fact it is my experience that almost every golfer I know, including me, could score better than they do without making any changes at all in their physical game. Do you doubt that? OK, let's talk about doubt.

Just before we do let me encourage you to believe in yourself, and let others know you believe in yourself, and your shots and your scores will most likely reflect that belief.

* * *

PUTTING IT INTO PLAY

We are a curious lot, aren't we? From 1963 to somewhere around the 1990's, one of the most popular answers to "What's the first thing you'll ask when you get to heaven?" was "Who shot JFK?" The producers and writers of a TV show called *Dallas* knew that and played on it with a curiosity plot of their own, "Who shot JR?"

When you get to heaven, and I sincerely hope you do, who shot JFK will not be on your mind. If there is any mental activity once the overwhelming joy subsides a bit, it will be surprise—surprise that some are there you didn't think would be, surprise that some are missing you were sure would be there, and the biggest surprise of all, that you are there. But I digress.

Our curious nature not only makes us want to answer the mysteries of the past, it makes us want to know the future.

It's part of the reason why we look up when we hit a golf ball, and it's a big part of the reason why we constantly calculate our score as we play a round of golf.

If we could eliminate that particular curiosity and use the energy for either relaxation or focus, we'd be far better off.

A story is coming about Byron Nelson and not knowing your score before you shoot it, but the place to start with this is at the turn. Do not let your scorekeeper, even if that is you, tell you what you shot on the front or even ask you if that agrees with what you thought you shot. You might even need to tell your fellow competitors before you start that you don't want to know your score. Besides, what you shot on the front doesn't matter—what you shoot for 18 matters. The first half of a movie can be great and the last half can be terrible. Is that a "thumbs up" movie? No.

Focus on each shot, not on the score. Get your mind out of future mode and into present mode, and let someone else add up the numbers. You'll be surprised at how low the score can be if you just leave it alone and let it happen.

7

No Doubt

There is a well-known passage in the Bible where a man
is asking Jesus to cast a demon out of his son "if he can."
Jesus says to him "If I can? All things are possible to him who
believes." To which the man replied, "Lord, I believe. Help
my unbelief."

Have you ever felt like that before hitting a golf shot?

Doubt is a place on the road between belief and unbelief.
In the Greek text (the New Testament was written origi-
nally in Greek) the words above for belief and unbelief are
the same, except the second word begins with an "a," which
means without. For instance, a theist is one who believes God
exists while an atheist does not believe God exists. I don't
know anyone who claims to be a theist one day and an atheist
the next and a theist the next, but golfers do it all the time.

"I can hit this bunker shot."

"Last time you hit a bunker shot it was thin and it went over the green."

"I'm hitting this one just right. I've got this."

"But that thin shot was embarrassing."

To doubt is to waver. People who doubt have not made up their minds—they are of two minds and are wavering between them. There are generally two ways this shows up in a round of golf, and neither one is likely to help your score. Here is what they look like and how you can deal with them.

The first and least insidious way, but still bad, is to waver between two opinions on a shot. This can happen on almost any shot, but often happens on short putts.

The conversation between your two minds goes like this.

"Hit it firmly and take the break out of it."

"No, hit it easy and let it break into the hole."

Either would be fine, but what usually happens is you play the break and hit it firmly and the ball races past the hole, allowing the conversation to begin anew.

Plant a tree in the fairway

At the club my brother belonged to in Virginia (and the phrase has now been spread throughout Arizona) they refer to a shot hit without a clear mind as an HIA, which stands for "hit it anyway." You have done that and so have I, and the results are rarely good.

One of the most common causes of an HIA is doubt about what shot I'm going to hit. Allow me to contrast that with a different scenario.

A shot I am almost always likely to hit well, and perhaps

this applies to you, is a shot with limited options. For instance I find myself in light rough 120 yards from the center of the green (a wedge for me) but with a tree about ten yards in front of me. It is just close enough and tall enough that I can't get over the highest part with more than a sand-wedge, and there is water in front of the green that keeps me from landing it short or running it on. Fortunately there is a small gap on the top right of the tree that is low enough for my wedge to clear.

I still have options, of course. I can pitch out into the fairway, or I can call an unplayable lie and take a drop or replay the shot. But hitting it through that gap is not that risky as long as I focus, and focus I do.

Doubt between shots never enters the equation, and that is a big part of the reason that better players hit some of their best shots when they are "in trouble" on the course.

One way to overcome the kind of doubt that wonders which shot you should hit (toward the water on the right with a draw back into the fairway, or starting left away from the water with a fade into the fairway?) is to plant a tree in the path of one of those options. Or build a bunker if you prefer, but create something in your mind on the golf course that forces you to limit your choices to one, then focus on that choice and hit the shot. The good news is that an imaginary tree is fairly easy to hit through, just in case.

Over the years I've tried this tactic with success with a number of players, and it is surprisingly easy to incorporate. The power behind it is that it stops the wavering, causes you to focus more precisely, and gives you a shot to hit.

I think I can, I think I can, I think I can

I can still picture the bedroom my brother and I shared in our childhood home where I first read *The Little Engine That Could*. I probably need to re-read that classic before I head out to the golf course, because it might help prevent some of the other kind of doubt.

The doubt I speak of here is the worst kind of all—self-doubt, and some days it seems you have to be a combination of The Little Engine and Norman Vincent Peale (*The Power of Positive Thinking*) to keep it at bay. Incredible talent and a Hall of Fame record are insufficient barriers to self-doubt creeping into your game. Those are certainly helpful, but all you have to do is look at the different putting grips, strokes and putters themselves on the PGA Tour to know that self-doubt has affected some of the best in the world. This enemy requires special tactics.

From a practical perspective, and that is what we are about here, the question is, "When it shows up how can I get rid of it, and what do I do in the meantime?"

Here is one way a world-class player dealt with self-doubt in chipping in real time in an incredibly challenging situation. (You will notice, by the way, that self-doubt is often heightened with the level of the challenge before you.)

I exchanged a few e-mails not long ago with a man named Pete Oakley who won the Senior British Open in 2004. That is an extraordinary accomplishment, and he did it as a Monday qualifier. He is still the only qualifier to win that major, as far as I know, and he clearly is a great player. He beat some other great players coming down the stretch, including both

Eduardo Romero and Hall of Famer Tom Kite, who tied for second one shot back. And he did all that without ever hitting a chip shot or pitch shot from a tight lie.

He just couldn't get his mind around the possibility that he might miss one of those shots, so he used his putter everywhere he could. He doubted that he could hit a chip/pitch from a tight lie, so he didn't even attempt to do so. He eliminated one side of the argument, and it worked.

There is no shame at all in doing this, so if you doubt that you can hit a driver into the fairway, don't hit it. If you doubt your ability to hit a long par three green in regulation, lay up and play for bogey or a possible par. All of that is better than fighting doubt, which will drive you absolutely bonkers.

A second way to temporarily defeat self-doubt in real time is to shut the door in its face. That is, do not let it enter your conscious thinking. Thankfully there is a relatively simple way to keep it out, and that is by giving your attention to something else.

Target, not technique

Technique is very important in golf. Please don't let anything I say here make you think otherwise. In the short game, in the long game, in putting, proper technique will make it easier to make solid and consistent contact, and it will make your efforts more efficient.

Of course there are many ways to putt, many ways to chip, and many ways to hit a bunker shot. Your technique may be unique to you, or it may be a carbon copy of one of the best players ever; it doesn't really matter. What does matter is that you must believe in your technique enough to ignore it when you are hitting a shot for score.

Doubting your technique is not only understandable, sometimes it is appropriate. I went through a fairly long spell like that not so long ago, and I could not find my way back. Did I take a lesson? Not really. Over time I did ask a few friends to take a look at my chipping technique (that was where the issue was), and at least one of those was a teaching pro. I video-recorded my chipping so I could see what was happening, and I spent a lot of time practicing chipping, sometimes even on a tee while I was waiting on the group in front of us.

Can you see where the problem was? I never trusted my technique. When the shot didn't count I was a pretty solid chipper. In the round I was well below average.

Doubt wasn't making any of this better, but I never, ever doubted that I would resolve the issue and get back the short game that had helped keep my scores low in the past.

In the middle of all that I attended a golf lecture that was being conducted by Stan Utley, whom I had met, and E. A. Tischler, whom I had not met. Stan is known throughout the golf world as one of the best short-game instructors anywhere, and E.A. is a bio-mechanics expert and outstanding teacher.

After the lecture I reminded Stan that I would be seeing him in a few days for a lesson with three of my friends, and I also told him I hoped he was part psychologist because I was having mental issues with my chipping.

"It's not mental," he said, "It's technique."

He had never seen me hit a chip shot, so how could he be so sure?

A few days later I found out he was at least partly right, my technique had become flawed. It wasn't a big fault, which is why I could get away with it much of the time and why my friends and I had such a hard time seeing it, but it was enough to cause problems.

The times when I chipped the very best were the times when I just focused on the target and didn't think about the technique, but when the stakes were higher I would lose the flow of my routine, take too much time over the ball, let doubt creep in while the target faded from my mind, and have poor results.

My point is that even while my technique was a bit broken I should have trusted it during play. If I had listened to my own advice of "target, not technique" I would have been far better off, but I yielded to the temptation to try to fix it while I was playing and I suffered for it.

One more line that might have helped, given that I was certainly taking too long over the shots I doubted, was spoken by George Duncan, the 1920 Open Champion who was well known for his fast play and for being "the pro's pro" because he was a great teacher as well as a great player. Duncan said, "If you're going to miss 'em, miss 'em quick."

There isn't much time to think about failure when you play like Duncan played, assessing the situation and planning his shot as he walked up to the ball, then standing to one side and swinging.

I've played like that in a couple of golf marathons (100 holes in a day), and to be honest with you it is not all that bad. I'd rather have a moment to look at the lie and do some more thinking and visualizing, but if I could train myself to do that more efficiently as I approach the ball I would certainly play faster. And I probably wouldn't have time to worry over shots that didn't need to be worried over.

The secret is to get your conscious mind off to one side and out of the way, to not care much about results, and to simply let yourself hit the shot.

Get your "thinking" mind off the possibility of failure (or likelihood of failure, if doubt has you deeply in its grip) by giving it something else to think about, which I recommend being your target. If that is a chip shot, it may be a spot on the green. If it is a long iron or drive it may be a tree off in the distance. If it is a putt it might be a spot you want to roll the ball over.

Keep your conscious mind busy with that important job and let your body, which you have trained for this moment, execute the shot it knows in its gut it can execute. And do it quickly, before the bad thoughts know you've stopped to hit the ball.

I have no doubt you can do that.

* * *

PUTTING IT INTO PLAY

Of all the mental demons that can wander into a golf game (or even into life), doubt may be the most insidious and the most vile. This is not some cute little imp standing on your shoulder and arguing openly with an angel, this is a creepy guy who is poking a hot iron into your brain and calling your abilities into question.

In golf he can sneak into your psyche a dozen different ways, for instance floating in when a little breeze comes up and you suddenly say to yourself, "I don't know if this is enough club now." Or he might come out of the ground when you are taking a practice chip and you hit the ground a little too hard, or when you walk into a bunker and look up at the tall face of it in front of you.

He has just as many devious methods in life. One day Doubt might disguise himself as a well-meaning teacher, and on another he might try to get you to compare yourself to a super-star. Even if you listen, do not believe.

When you feel doubt creeping in you should acknowledge it, but you should not give in to it. If the sudden breeze makes you stop and think, stop and think and then commit to a shot and hit it. If your practice chip was a little chunky, be glad it was a practice chip, focus on the target rather than that inconsequential practice swing and then hit the chip.

Preparation helps immensely in keeping doubt away, but he can still get in. Look him in the eye when he does and say, "I know you for who you are. Now get out of here while I hit this shot with trust and commitment." He won't stay long.

8

Perfection

This will be a fairly short chapter, but coming right after "Doubt" is a good place for it. Here is something you should never doubt: you cannot achieve perfection in golf.

Sure, you can try. You can hit thousands of balls and you can hit two-hundred putts and you can hit a hundred bunker shots a day and... wait, why would you ever hit a bunker shot if you had perfection in your drives and irons? Just for the occasional bad bounce? No, since you're going to be perfect you might as well stay out of the sand.

And while you're at it don't ever practice hitting the ball wrong sided (lefty if you're a righty) or escaping from trouble in some other way because, well, you just won't be in trouble.

Of course you will, as has been every player who ever played the game or ever will, and that is part of the joy of it all. You will make mistakes in your setup, in your tempo, in your swing, and in the choices you make on the course. And it is entirely possible that you will make all of those mistakes within a single round, though probably not within a single shot. (I've come close.)

The goal is to have a great setup, wonderful tempo, a swing that is yours, and the flexibility to adapt to changing conditions including turf, grain, pressure and weather, among others. The goal is not and should not be perfection.

Recently I heard Freddy Jacobsen, former European Tour player and for several years now a full-time member of the PGA Tour, say, "I gave up trying to be perfect in my game a long time ago." He laughed as he said it, realizing that he had tried for that impossible goal early in his career and that he understood now how silly that was.

In fact Tour players will tell you that somewhere around 50% of their shots in any given round come off almost exactly as they intended them to. One of the great players of the past—I think it was Walter Hagen—said he only hit about seven really pure shots in a normal round.

The potential danger of striving for perfection

I remember playing a round of golf with my future boss at his club near San Francisco a number of years ago. Wanting to impress him with my game I tried a little too hard and didn't play particularly well. I was trying to make perfect swings and I knew it, but I couldn't stop. Then I got into a little trouble on a par four.

The course was hilly, and my ball was probably ten feet below and to the side of the putting surface on a sloping lie. I could see the top half of the flagstick, only fifteen yards away. Suddenly I couldn't think about perfection because the challenge of the shot before me demanded all my attention.

Because I was focused my instincts took over, my game went on automatic, and I hit the shot of the day with the ball flying high, landing softly, and stopping just a few feet from the hole. I remember my boss-to-be saying, "No pro could have hit that shot any better."

I wanted to say that they probably wouldn't need to hit it at all because they wouldn't be where I was in the first place, but instead I just said, "Thanks."

The differences between the pros and us are these: While I might have one or two really excellent shots in a round, they have six or seven or eight. And while my misses are usually fairly easy to identify as misses, their misses look very much like good shots. In fact you can tell that you are getting better when your misses begin to consistently turn out well.

"But," someone will ask, "if I strive for perfection but don't reach it, won't I still get better at golf anyway?" It's that old "aim for the stars and hit the moon" kind of thing. I'm going to take a bit of a risk here and say, "Not necessarily."

It is true that the more you strive to improve some golf skill the more likely it is that you will improve. That means you will have more skill in that area, and that may, but doesn't always, translate into what you called making you "better at golf." Being better at golf shot doesn't always equate to better at golf.

If you've been reading carefully you will already understand that improving a skill in one area of your physical game can take a lot of time and effort. It only makes sense that while you are focusing on that area, other areas are getting less attention and may therefore diminish, or at least atrophy.

If I lift weights (Hey, it could happen!) and focus on my arms but neglect my legs, my strength will improve in one place and get worse in another.

So striving for perfection in a golf swing can actually cause your scores to go up, at least temporarily, because the singular focus on that area takes time away from other areas. The danger is, those neglected areas may take a long time to heal, or they could even be permanently scarred.

A lesson from a golf hustler

There is a second reason why striving for perfection might hurt you, and it has to do with practicality—what works and what doesn't. Here's how that affects golf and how you might apply it. And why I know it.

At some point along the journey called golf, your swing will be at its peak. The problem is, you are not likely to accept that fact even if you recognize it. Your goal—if you find that place—is to try to maintain it for as long as you can; your goal is not to make it better, but to make it permanent.

It may not be better than someone else's swing, but it is as good as your swing has ever been and it is right for you. If you try to add something to it, it will get worse rather than improving. When you see the first sign of this, jettison the thing you were trying to do to make it better and hope that it didn't do any lasting damage.

Remember this point: your swing is to be desired over an idealized perfect swing. Ask Lee Trevino, ask Jim Furyk, ask

Arnold Palmer.

Speaking of Arnold Palmer, are you familiar with the ad campaign where he says, "Swing your swing?" He's right, because while your swing may not be "perfect" in the sense of hitting every position, it is much more likely to be effective than any other swing. The more you mess with it, the less effective it will be.

A little over two years ago I was playing a casual round with a fellow who himself was fairly round, but the man could play golf. His swing was a little strange looking, partly to accommodate "Middle Girth," but his action through the ball was excellent. It was obvious to me by the second hole that this was not his first rodeo, and, partly because I had been involved in some golf hustling as a teenager, my antennae were up for him to propose a wager.

He had already told me his regular set of clubs had been stolen out of his truck, which was why he happened to be using an old set that he didn't like as well. And there were apparently other challenges he was facing that were going to make it more difficult for him to play well that day.

I knew that part of the hustle on a golf course is to make yourself look vulnerable. If you look invincible, no one will bet with you.

By the fourth tee he was mentioning a golf guru of the past, talking swing theory, and complimenting me on my knowledge of the game and its history.

Another part of the hustle is to make the victim (me, in this case) over-confident. There was a brief pause in the conversation and then he said, "Do you ever like to play for a little something?"

Knowing this was coming I was able to side-step it. I said that a long time ago I had been known to gamble on golf, but not any longer. I also told him, truthfully, that I was working on my swing. Thankfully he didn't push it but instead decided he would help me a little. He started by encouraging me to forget the stuff I was working on, and he didn't even know what that was.

When we reached the seventh tee, a short par 3 of about 165 yards, he said, "You've obviously been playing pretty good golf for a pretty long time. What was your swing like before you started trying to fix it?"

I suddenly got a picture in my mind—or was it a feeling in my bones?—about that rhythmic swing of mine, stood on the tee, and promptly hit the ball to within two feet of the hole. I kept that swing for the next two holes, and at the turn my new coach quit, pleading some previous appointment. I saw him an hour or so later across a couple of fairways, and I hoped he was making a little spending cash.

That lesson is one of the best I ever got, and it turns out that even the pros understand it and apply it. Of course they are playing at a far different level and for far different reasons, and many of them have professional coaches who can help them make small adjustments in their swings. After all, even the tiniest incremental improvement can be worth tens of thousands of dollars in a season, which could easily make the difference between keeping your job or losing it. But most of us should mostly leave it alone. Even professionals who are smart don't think about making changes until their off season.

Should you make corrections now and then? Of course. If your grip has moved or if your alignment is off or even if your swing plane has changed, fix those things. But be very, very careful about undertaking adjustments that will fundamentally change the way you swing a golf club, especially if you're doing it because you think it looks better. Trevino, Furyk and Palmer all understand that their paychecks have never been determined by the beauty of the swing, and they have all done just fine, thank you.

Follow their lead and skip the search for perfection. Just find your swing, because it may well be perfect for you.

* * *

PUTTING IT INTO PLAY

I am a tweaker and a fiddler when it comes to golf, and I know it and fight it. Thankfully my swing and my putting stroke have mostly survived these generally ill-advised and ill-fated attempts to make them better. But my chipping suffered terribly.

All it took was listening to someone speak with great authority in a short-game clinic, and I thought, "I should chip like this guy." Honestly I didn't really know how I chipped at the time, but he was so convincing that I was sure this would make me unstoppable. I was apparently already capable, because I shot in the 60s often and never once worried about having to get up and down from anywhere around the green. Naturally I missed some of those attempts, but it was never a worry for me.

I'll skip the horrid history of the chipping saga and tell you that it was like this: imagine walking down a street in a large city and finding your way just fine when someone you don't know comes out of a store and says, "You're going the wrong way, Friend. I'm the expert on this town. You need to turn left down the next street, go three-and-a-half blocks, turn right at the alley, go through the first blue door you see (it's the back of a Chinese restaurant), go up the stairs to the roof, jump over to the building on the west, go downstairs and through the building out on to the street. That's the best way to get where you want to be."

You wouldn't do it, because you'd get lost. So why do you do what some unknown person tells you to do about your swing—or your chipping?

If you need directions, consult a known source. If you need help with some aspect of your swing, go to a professional teacher that you know or who is recommended by someone you know. The attitude you should listen for is that he or she wants to take your swing and make it as good as it can be. You do not want someone who says, "My way or the highway."

Do you want to read tips and instructional articles in magazines? Fine, but then file them away in your mind and do not attempt to incorporate them into your game unless they include some very specific point that you already know is an issue for you.

Perfection is not achievable in life (which is why we need grace) or golf. All attempts to become perfect at golf cause you to end up in the back of a Chinese restaurant, wondering how in the world you ever got there.

9

A Little Risky

Even the best players in the world rarely play a complete round of golf without having to decide whether or not to try some risky shot. Those who set up the course and choose the pin placements see to that, so risk assessment is involved even when we are playing well. On days when our game is less under control than on other days, a simple chip shot over a bunker might be risky.

Give a Tour player a tucked-back-right-with-water-just-off-the-green pin position on a day when she is hitting the ball with complete confidence and success, and that pin may look like it is in the middle of wide open spaces. Give her the same shot on a day when she's already missed three shots to the right and a fish pond will look like the raging North Atlantic Ocean. In scenario one the risk is small, in scenario two it is almost insurmountable.

One important factor in both scenarios, though, is that she has actually assessed the risk. Amateur golfers rarely do so, and when they do they rarely assess it based on their game that day.

That is because most amateur golfers have hit a number of very good shots in their playing career, and they often assume they will do so again when faced with a "risky" shot. I applaud the optimism, but this may not be the best application of that marvelous trait.

There are a several elements at work here, along with a multiplying factor, so grab your calculator.

Risk assessment

Most amateurs I know walk up to a ball measuring the distance to the target. Distance must be determined, but it is only one factor and it is not even the most important factor. That distinction belongs to the lie of the ball.

I once wrote a daily devotion for Links Players International titled, First, consider the lie. In it I told the story of a former PGA Tour player I caddied for at our club a few times when I was a young teenager. He explained to me that the lie of the ball often dictated what kind of shot you could hit, and that nothing else really mattered much until you figured that out. If the lie was good and clean and relatively flat there were more options, but if the ball was in a divot or on the side of a hill or sitting down in the rough, the options might be limited. He said it was no good figuring out the distance to the green if you couldn't hit it there, so not to worry about that until you saw how the ball was sitting.

Now it may be that your ability level can overcome an awkward lie. I once saw a pro I was playing with hit a twenty-yard hook around a palm tree and over water from the left rough with the ball well below his feet. Most of us could not have done that, but he assessed it, knew his abilities, and was able to hit the shot.

Still, that shot was not as dramatic as Bubba Watson's famous forty-yard hook with a gap wedge out of the trees from 165 yards in the playoff for the 2012 Masters.

(I happened to see Champions Tour player Don Pooley not long after "the Bubba shot" and he asked me if I could curve a gap-wedge forty yards. I said that I could not. He agreed, noting that very few people who are not Bubba Watson can generate enough club head speed with a gap wedge to turn it that much.)

So the second thing to consider, and we've been talking about it already, is your ability. How good are you from a hanging lie? How good are you out of divot? How good are you off the dirt? How good are you out of thick rough? How good are you at hitting the ball high or low or to the right or left (on purpose, I mean)? Here is where brutal honesty will save you strokes. You may believe in yourself to the very hilt, but if you have not practiced hitting the ball high or low or curving it a certain amount, in the middle of a round is probably not the time to start.

More importantly, how good are you at all those things that day?

A basketball coach has to decide who gets the ball for the last shot, and usually it goes to the player who has the hot hand. Optimism and confidence are terrific qualities to have, but even those must be tempered by what is happening in real time. If your A-game is not with you, think carefully before you try what is for you an A-game shot.

Getting to scratch is not about a great round or two, though that will help. It is about consistently shooting low scores. You will only do that if you consider your abilities on every shot, and if you are aware that your abilities ebb and flow.

The third factor is the path between the ball and the target. If it is an approach shot and you are in the fairway, trees are less likely to intervene, although they can. Water may be in the way, as may grass or sand bunkers or false fronts or other architectural deviations designed to make the shot more challenging. You must note which of these are present, although you don't need to dwell on them.

One word about hitting it over trees, since we are there. A quick way to determine whether your club has enough loft to clear the tree is to let the club show you. To do this, back away from the ball a few feet and lay the club down on the ground with the handle pointing toward the target (and the intervening tree) with the face of the club facing the sky. Now step on the blade of the club so that the handle points up in the air. That will show you the angle of the flight of the ball, and it is quite easy to visualize whether or not you have enough loft. It's even legal, but be careful in this process (and always) not to do anything that even gives the appearance of altering the ground around your ball.

Your target is probably not the goat

OK, you've considered the lie, your ability, and the intervening path. The final step is to select a target you have a reasonable chance of hitting. That might be the middle of the green, even if the pin isn't there. Here is an important point and one that is universally agreed to by every excellent player: Do not automatically aim at the flag.

(Remember that advice on practicing target? Now is the time to apply it.)

A college coach once had his team play an entire round with all the flags removed from the greens, and the results surprised his players in a positive way. Try it yourself someday if you can arrange it, and if you can't then try to play a complete round aiming your approach shot at the middle of every green regardless of where the flag is. Odds are that your score will come down if you have the discipline to try just that one thing.

Once the target is selected, decide how you want to get the ball to it. Do you want to hit it high or low or curving or straight? Whatever you choose, it is important that you have all that in mind before you address the ball. Some people call this process visualization, some call it painting a picture. Call it what you will, but do not ignore it, even if you think you can't do it yet.

In my case, I don't dwell on this picture for any length of time. There is enough slow play without me getting lost in the moment while I admire a shot I'm playing in my mind. I then look at the target, and as long as I'm committed to that target, it can basically be just a glance. No staring contest is involved, and there should also be no doubt. What you put in your mind is the odds on favorite for where the ball will go.

This known fact is, of course, why unscrupulous partners of yours will try to get you to look at the water or the trees or a bunker. Do not let them succeed. Those things may be there, and it is fine to acknowledge their presence, but your eyes should go to your target, not their suggestions.

In the late 1940's a man named Ivan McAllister was one of the best players at our little club, and he won the club championship several times. Back then the management also kept a couple of goats on the course to help keep the rough lower. It was cheap labor, and kind of a nice tip of the cap to the sheep of Scotland that helped shape so many courses.

Anyway, Ivan and his opponent were on the first tee for the finals of the club championship, according to my father, and as Ivan teed up, the opponent noticed that one of the goats was in the left rough about 200 yards out. In a very helpful tone he said, "Ivan, don't hit that goat." My dad said the first sound he heard was the crack of the ball on the club face, and the next sound he heard was, "Baaaaaaaaaaaa!" Ivan had hit the goat square in the side.

He never recovered (Ivan, that is—the goat was fine) and went on to lose the match. He also proved the power of the mind to direct our muscles to achieve a particular end, like hitting a golf ball at a target. If your mind/body will do that for you, let me suggest you pick a target you want to hit. And I hope it is not a goat.

One important note on Ivan and "Don't hit that goat," which sounds a lot like "Don't hit it in the water," "Don't hit it out-of-bounds left," and other similar statements.

Your mind dismisses the word "don't" in those scenarios and believes you are telling it to hit the goat, the water, or out-of-bounds left. For some reason all our mind does with such talk is focus on the named target.

What is the antidote for this? First you have to acknowledge the directive and then you have to dismiss it and then you have to replace it.

The formula is pretty simple, and it might play out something like this:

"Ivan, don't hit that goat."

(Ivan, as he backs away from the shot:) "Thanks, Partner. I hadn't noticed the goat before."

Now Ivan is in his process again, has dismissed the goat, and he is acquiring the target he does want to hit. That makes the goat happy.

* * *

PUTTING IT INTO PLAY

The secret here is to have a mental process that includes at least the following four elements. You may add one or two of your own, but you should not eliminate any of these: consider the lie, consider your ability that day, check the intervening path, and pick a target that incorporates the first three elements in its selection.

You make this process part of your pre-shot routine the same way you do everything else—by committing to it and practicing it. If you have to write it down on the scorecard, write it down, but do not forget it and do not fail to employ it.

Remember, this process only works if you are honest with yourself about your ability on that day at that moment. You might be in a big tournament and nervous, or you might be completely relaxed. You might be having a great day or a bad one. It all matters. And if you can do all of that, you will find that you are soon hitting your shots with far more confidence. The risk will have been reduced, and your results will be better for it.

In the same way, it is important for us to be honest with ourselves as we consider the risks presented to us in life. Those might be financial risks, relationship risks, career risks or even safety risks. If you are like me, you've encountered all of those.

Do I have a process for assessing the risk properly? For most of my life I didn't, but thanks to thinking about this in golf I figured I should find one or create one, and it has proven to be very helpful.

One thing it has in common with my golf process is step one: First, consider the lie. Satan is a liar and the father of lies, according to the Bible. So the first thing to check in some potentially risky situation is whether or not some kind of lie is involved. That will go a long way toward reducing the number and severity of the risks you encounter. Remember, the truth will set you free.

10

It's All About The Flat Stick

The first time I became a scratch player I was in my early twenties and serving my country as a soldier in South Korea. My actual job in the Army had to do with secret-message machines, which was fun, and I liked the guys I worked with.

Our shop was manned 24 hours a day every day and we worked in shifts of eight or more hours. There was barbed wire around our area and that kept out most of the officers and gave those of us inside a lot of flexibility, as long as we did our work well and in a timely manner.

There also happened to be a U.S. owned golf course on the

base where I was stationed. It was within walking distance of the Quonset hut I lived in, and play was incredibly cheap, so when spring broke in Korea I asked my dad to send my clubs to me, which he did.

Not many soldiers who were enlisted men, like me, played at the 8th Army HQ course, and in fact I don't recall the place ever being overly crowded, but I showed up almost every day for the two or three warm months I was stationed at Camp Coiner. I still did my real job, but I spent many hours on that golf course.

I had no distractions in those days other than work, so I dedicated myself to playing the game. I played almost every day, practiced a great deal when I wasn't playing, and I thought very little when I was playing. I also played occasionally with and against some excellent players, which is always good for one's game.

One of those players was Bob Eastwood. Like me, he was a soldier. Unlike me, his assigned job was to work at the golf course. He got that assignment, I assume, because of his skill with a golf club. In fact when he got out of the Army he went straight to Q-School for the PGA Tour, finished first, and then kept his Tour membership for many years.

Although we played several rounds of golf together, I mostly saw Bob on the putting green. He worked hard with "the flat stick" and was an excellent putter. Part of what inspired him was that he had once been in a practice-green putting contest with Sam Snead, and Snead (an inveterate gambler) had bet Bob he could putt with his foot better than the young man could putt with his putter. I don't know who won, but the result was that Bob was very serious about putting.

Some ten or twelve years after my time in Korea I was living in the Chicago area, and I went to the Western Open golf tournament. In no small part my reason for going was to watch Bob and potentially say hello to him.

As he came off the 18th green after the second round and headed toward the scorer's tent, I was able to get close enough to greet him. After we re-established our golf connection from Korea, I asked him how it was out there on the Tour. He said, "It's all about the flat stick. Everybody can hit the ball, but not everybody can get it in the hole."

The fact that it is "all about the flat stick" may not seem like much of a revelation to you, but if you go to any practice area on any public golf course anywhere in America, the number of people practicing putting (not just hitting a few putts before their round) will be dwarfed by the number of people practicing the full swing.

Golf commentators and even golfers often say that putting is the difference-maker in scoring, but golfers everywhere treat that valuable piece of information with something short of disdain. I know this because I too am guilty of spending too little of my practice time rolling the ball in spite of the fact that I have a perfectly good area to practice putting just steps away in my garage.

Because this book isn't about how to hit a golf ball, even with a putter, I'll only say that what is true of any stroke is true of putting. An excellent setup, including posture, grip, aim and alignment, a tempo that is ingrained and the same on every putt, and a repeatable swing that puts the club head on the ball square to the line with sufficient energy are all desirable. But there are other things you should know about putting, and you should focus on them as well when you are practicing.

You may have even heard some of these more detailed putting thoughts, but I'm going to repeat them anyway in the hope that they'll make an impression on your game.

Putting advice 1

Distance is more important than line.

There is a long-standing debate among putting aficionados between "die it in the hole" and "hit it seventeen inches past the hole." Two of the best putters of all time, Bobby Jones and Jack Nicklaus, were primarily "die it in the hole" putters.

Even in Bob Jones' time people talked about the idea of hitting it past the hole, not because they had the scientific data that Dave Pelz has put together, but because they knew that a putt that stayed short never went in.

When confronted with that information, usually as a question about his style, Bobby Jones is said to have answered, "But I never saw a putt that was long go in, either."

And that is closer to the heart of this matter. A putt that is left short but close to the hole is a two-putt and not a one-putt, but it is also not a three-putt.

If you can get the ball to stop 17 inches past the hole or if you can get the ball to stop one inch from the hole, you will lead the league in three-putt avoidance.

Line is important, and we'll discuss that in more depth shortly, but you are far more likely to three-putt because of poor distance control than you are poor line. If you want to score well, three-putt holes need to be reduced dramatically and in most rounds eliminated completely.

Professional golfers can and should spend time lining up putts in competition because they already know how far they are going to hit it. (Yes, there are exceptions.)

Those of us who aspire to break 90 or 80 or 70 need to know about reading greens, but we need to spend much more time on the practice green learning how to control distance than we do learning how to read the line.

We generally all have a better and more natural eye for line than we give ourselves credit for. Every day we walk through door ways, we get into cars, we successfully navigate our bodies into chairs, we walk down streets and somehow avoid bumping into each other.

We cut out coupons, we drive cars and ride bicycles, we pick up forks and use them to lift food to our mouths, and we succeed more than 99% of the time. All of those are akin to reading the line of a putt, so you've been practicing that general skill for most of your life.

OK, I'll stop preaching now and tell you that there are a number of ways to practice distance control in putting, but a prerequisite for consistent distance control is consistent contact with the ball.

Go get your putter, and grab it just below the grip with the thumb and forefinger of your left hand, then hold it up in the air so that the face of the putter is about eye-level in front of you, hanging like the pendulum of a grandfather clock.

With the tip of the forefinger of your free hand, tap the center of the putter face—the place that is supposed to be "the sweet spot." You will notice that the putter swings almost straight back when you do that, and notice also that the putter head doesn't twist at all.

Now take a little talcum powder and sprinkle it on your putter face, then hit a putt and examine the contact point. (You can do this in your house or garage. No hole is required.) Ideally the "empty spot" where the putter hit the ball will be on or near the center of the putter face, but what is most important is that it is consistent. So now that you have this figured out, go ahead and hit a few more putts (refreshing the powder as needed) then examine your contact points.

The reason consistent contact is so important is not because a ball struck other than on the sweet spot is likely to go astray, it is because a ball struck like that will go a shorter distance than one struck perfectly.

Which raises this question: How do you know how far you hit a putt if you don't know where on the face you hit the putt? It makes a definite difference, which you can easily demonstrate to yourself by hitting a few putts.

There are any number of ways to learn to hit your putts on the sweet spot, or very close to it, and of course there are some excellent putters with inserts that greatly minimize the loss of distance on putts hit off the sweet spot.

Try any or all or none of that, but without fail you must come to understand that your primary task on every putt is to hit it the proper distance. In my own putting routine, the very last thing I do is look at the place I want the ball to finish while saying to myself, "Hit it that far." Then I look at the ball and stroke it. It's amazing how accurate my computer (brain) is, though it is no more amazing than yours.

Want to see how brilliant your brain is? Toss a ball to a friend. Throw a piece of crumpled paper at a wastebasket. You can do both of those things accurately without thinking because you are looking at the target and simply reacting to it.

I try to do that same thing with my putting routine, and it works.

Remember that to score well on and around the greens distance is king and direction is queen, while from the tee to the green direction is king and distance is queen. Most of us have that backwards, and getting it right if you have it wrong is guaranteed to save you strokes.

Of course in both the long and short games, the ideal is to keep the king and the queen happy. The right direction with the right distance yields the best result, but on the greens distance control is critical to good scoring.

Putting advice 1a

Speed determines line.

In a few paragraphs we'll talk about gravity, but even without thinking of gravity you already know that a ball that is rolling faster on a green breaks lesss than a ball that is rolling slower. That leads us to two important things to remember on the greens.

First, on any putt that is 18 feet or longer, you should read the break in thirds. Honestly I don't know if 18 feet is the right number, but it is divisible by three so let's use it.

The first 6 feet of an 18 foot putt won't be greatly affected by the slope because it will be rolling too fast.

The second 6 feet of an 18 foot putt will be affected more

because the ball is slowing down.

The last 6 feet will be affected the most, because the ball is traveling the slowest.

So when you are looking at the line, think about the speed the ball will be rolling when it gets to a particular part of the green, and pay more attention to the break around the hole than you do to the break at the beginning of the putt.

If your putt is shorter, you may divide it in half instead of in thirds. If it is very short and uphill, you may not divide it at all. But always think of the break relative to speed.

Someone sent Stan Utley a putting training aid that beautifully demonstrates the speed/line ratio. About two feet tall and shaped like a ski jump, but with the base laying flat on the green rather than elevating, you place a ball at some point on the ramp, which is marked every 1/4 inch. When you release the ball it rolls down the slope and onto the green, going exactly where it was aimed.

He showed us that on a sloping putt of six feet, starting the ball 1/4 inch too high caused the putt to lip out on the high side, while starting it 1/4 inch too low caused it to miss on the low side.

After watching this for no more than five minutes I was amazed that anyone ever makes a putt longer than two feet!

The margins are very small indeed, and there is no question that changing the speed of a putt seriously changes the line.

Putting advice 2

Practice putting distance before you play.
You may never have heard of Edward S. Stimpson, the

1935 Massachusetts Amateur champion, but you probably know of his invention, the Stimpmeter. It measures the speed of a putting surface and the results of that measurement are given in numbers like 10 or 12 or 9. Most golfers don't know exactly what that means, but they do know that a higher number means faster greens.

The Stimpmeter is basically a 36-inch-long extruded-aluminum v-shaped bar with a notch in it at 30 inches. With the Stimpmeter flat on the ground a golf ball is placed in the notch and then that end of the bar is raised slowly until the weight of the ball causes is to slip out of the notch. The ball will then roll down the bar onto the green, roll for a bit, and eventually stop. That position is marked, the test is repeated twice more, and if all three results are within a few inches of each other, the average distance the ball rolled on the green is marked.

This series is then repeated going back toward the original starting point. Assuming the distance is consistent going both directions, the average of the two is taken and recorded as the speed of the green, expressed in feet.

According to the USGA, most American golf courses have greens that measure between 7 and 12. They also say that keeping greens above 10 on a consistent basis is not recommended because it can cause difficult-to-manage turf problems.

But how we golfers love to complain about slow greens and brag about playing greens that are very fast! We must be masochists at heart.

If you have excellent distance control with your putter, if you can learn to trust your mind to calculate the effort of the putt, and if you can get past the idea that "good" greens are always fast, it should make no difference to you whether the greens are an 8 or 50% faster at a 12. Unless you truly know how you putt on those exact readings, don't even ask. Just practice distance before you play.

I see a lot of golfers practicing putts of 6 to 10 feet before they head to the first tee. If you only have time to hit a few putts, my recommendation is that you hit two or three putts of 40 feet and learn the speed of the green. You don't even have to putt at a hole—putt at the fringe and try to stop the ball just before the fringe. Even if you choose a hole as your target, your goal is not to make a putt, your goal is to train your mind for distance control.

If you have time to hit some 3 or 4 foot putts, do that after you have figured out the distance. Leave the 10 or 12 foot putts alone before you play, because at this point you are not practicing putting, you are learning distance by hitting long putts and adding to your confidence by making several short putts.

Let's say you get to the first green and you have a 30 foot putt for birdie. It will seem relatively familiar and not all that daunting if you've just hit several 40 foot putts. And you already know that if you get it within 4 feet you've got a par in the bag. Good start!

One more word about distance control, and this is not only extremely valuable information for putting but it also applies to chip and pitch shots around the green.

Distance control in putts and chip/pitch shots is primarily achieved through rhythm. What that means is that all of your putts should have the same rhythm (a one - two count is useful here) and take the same amount of time.

How does the backswing and downswing of the putter on a two-foot putt take the same amount of time as the backswing and downswing of a twenty-foot putt? It's shorter, obviously, so it has to be slower. But you don't have to try to make it slower, just make it shorter and keep the same rhythm and it will naturally be slower.

Rhythm takes practice, as you might suspect, and one way to practice rhythm is with sound. If you have access to an electronic metronome (which you do if you have a smart phone or a tablet) set it at 60 beats per minute and see if you can putt by going back on the first beat and hitting the ball on the second beat. If that is too fast or slow for you, adjust the rhythm until it matches what is natural for you on a medium-length stroke (a ten or twelve foot putt).

In my case this helped immensely with short putts. For some reason I've always been a decent long putter, but sometimes my short putts would get a little "stabby." Keeping the rhythm has made those much smoother. And that has helped the rhythm of my heart.

Putting advice 3

See it go in, then watch it go in.

A number of years ago I was fortunate enough to take a short game lesson with Jim Flick, one of the nicest and most knowledgeable (and best) teachers the game has known. When we got to putting, Jim gave me a visual image that helped greatly.

He said, "Burn the putt into the hole."

What he meant by that—and this was especially useful on putts of twenty feet or less—is that I should imagine the line of the putt on fire, then roll the ball along the fire line. After a couple of tries, I was able to actually do that, and it was fun!

Other players I have talked to will use a white line on the ground (in their mind's eye), or a green line, or a red line, or a tiny little highway, but it is something they can see. I liked the idea of fire because it was "moving" and colorful and imagining it required focus, which kept it visible longer.

Whether you visualize a path or not, you will still find it helpful to "see" the ball go into the hole before you putt. You can see it go in with speed or just crawl over the edge, and that, too, will make a difference in your putt.

First, a quick word about testing your putting stroke. Put a shiny penny or a shiny dime on the ground two feet away from your ball and then putt your ball over that coin four times. If you can roll it over the coin three out of four times and come close on the fourth (or hit it), your alignment is consistent and your putting stroke is decent. If you can't do that, you probably have bad aim or bad alignment. If your aim and alignment are perfect and you still can't hit the coin three out of four times, you need to work on your stroke. Isn't that nice to know?

Now, back to visualizing a path and the ball going in the hole at some speed. This may sound a lot like some magic trick, but it is simply engaging the most powerful part of your body, your brain. Your muscles respond to the commands they are given by the brain, and most of those commands are not conscious commands. If they were, it would take you a long time to simply type an e-mail. Crossing your arms would be awkward. Eating a meal would be a chore. Making a good putting stroke would be almost impossible.

If you are focused on the line the ball needs to roll along, and if you have a reasonable putting stroke (do the test above), all you really need to do to make a lot of putts is have the distance (sweet spot and rhythm!), mentally see the ball go into the hole, hit the putt, and then watch it go in. Your mind is that powerful.

Putting advice 4

Drain your putts with better green reading.

Other than being struck by or striking another object, and for a putt that could include the putter, the hole, the flag stick, a ball mark or a pebble, among others, there is only one reason why a golf ball on a green rolls in one direction rather than another: gravity.

Technically gravity pulls a body (your golf ball, for instance, as well as you) toward the center of the earth. Often we simplify that and say that gravity pulls things down. Which means that a golf ball, which rolls easily on a putting surface because there is little frictional resistance, will naturally roll downhill and will require a force greater than gravity to make it roll uphill.

One object that shares this characteristic with a golf ball is water. If you poured a large bucket of water on a golf green, it would flow down hill every chance it got. In fact the reason that golf greens are built with slopes is at least partially to ensure that water, whether applied by God in the form of rain or by the staff through a hose or watering system, will run off the green and drain away.

By design, therefore, almost all "modern" greens have drains in the ground around them. Walk around a green next time you are on one and look for the drains. Some are more obvious than others, but they are almost always visible.

When you find the drains you know something about the green—you know which way it slopes. There are other ways to discover this, of course, the most common one being what is called reading the green.

Most people do that only with their eyes, but you should also read the slopes of greens with your feet, with the surroundings, and with your imagination.

Your feet are very sensitive and can almost always feel the changes in slope on a green. If you simply walk around your putt and pay attention you will feel the changes in slope and know whether your putt is uphill, downhill or sidehill.

Reading the surroundings in the Phoenix area is fairly simple for some courses. Phoenix is known as "the valley of the sun," and it truly is mostly in a valley that is surrounded by mountains. Because of gravity, everything wants to break toward the valley, which is downhill from the mountains.

Visually it's hard to believe that sometimes, and it even looks like some putts break uphill, but gravity is not to be defied, so pay attention to your surroundings.

Finally, read with your imagination. Pretend you are pouring water on the hole and watch where it flows. Imagine yourself bowling on the green and decide where the ball would roll. Look especially around the cup, because a slow moving ball has less power with which to defy gravity.

Ultimately you should make gravity your friend on the

green. Use it to let the ball roll naturally into the hole. I love that part of the game, and the more I love it the better I get at it. You will too, and you'll have a lot more fun working with gravity than against it.

* * *

PUTTING IT INTO PLAY

To review briefly, putting is extremely important in getting the ball in the hole. In fact almost every hole you play includes at least one putt.

But putting, as it turns out, is really less about the perfect stroke than it is about distance control, discovering the line, and visualization. All three of these are things that you can incorporate into your game immediately because they are skills you already possess.

Yes, you can improve them, and you should, but this is not hours of practice, it is just a matter of using them for about thirty minutes on a practice green, after which time you will be so amazed at how good you are that you'll be hooked.

And that is part of the reason they work so well—they both give your brain data to use in processing and they feed your belief, and your belief coupled with data improves your ability to "feel" distance (subconsciously) and "see" the path to the hole, which causes you to make more putts, which increases your belief and adds to the data.

This is a positive cycle, as you can see, and it has no upward limit. Every putt you hit, whether in practice or during a round, adds to your database. While it is true in virtually every worthy endeavor that "the more you know, the more you know you don't know," it is also true that "the more you know, the more you know."

Take advantage of that on the golf course and in the course of your day, storing information then retrieving it and applying what you have learned to the situation at hand. Do that both consciously and sub-consciously, relishing the opportunity to use your vast experience to make good decisions and create good outcomes.

As a bonus, it adds greatly to the fun.

11

Meet Your Mind

Bobby Jones said the only distance he consistently had trouble with in golf was the 5 ½ inches between his ears. I get that, and you probably do, too. In fact, while playing golf I have often identified with a tag line from a series of commercials that were aired years ago: "A mind is a terrible thing to waste."

In this chapter we'll look at several of the more common "mental" problems that can plague a golfer in his travels around the links. If you recognize any of these immediately, perhaps it's because you have played golf with me at some time. I have known them all.

Anger

Let's face it, golf can be a maddening game. It can drive

you crazy and it can make you angry. The former happens more often, but the player who gets a bad bounce after he hits a great shot and doesn't turn just a tiny bit red is the player who has his temper under control.

For the rest of us, the injustice of the bad bounce is often enough to make sweat beads pop out on our forehead. As we wipe those away we continue to fantasize about the great score that might have been if not for the evil nature of the golf gods, and by the time we reach our next shot our only focus is on what might have been rather than on what is. Our anger grows.

Hitting a golf shot in anger—whether you are mad at life, the aforementioned golf gods, your boss, or yourself—is a bad thing and simply should not be done. The Bible says to not let the sun go down on your anger, which is good advice, but in golf do not let anger reside in you for even the time it takes to get to your ball for the next shot—even if that ball is still where it was.

What is the antidote? What can you do when you feel anger creeping in? You can remember my pain, laugh at it, and choose not to experience it. Here's how it happened.

I was playing a nice little private course in the Bay Area of San Francisco, where we lived. My brother, father and step-mother had come out for a visit, so we had a fun foursome. My co-worker was a member, and he got us on the course but didn't join us.

One short par four had a fence to the left of the tee, with trees and wild shrubbery growing in the uncleared and hilly property that ran down into a valley. About 200 yards out, also on the left, was a pond. The fairway wrapped around it and went another 150 yards up to the green. Wanting to avoid the water, I hit a fairway wood off the tee.

This was a beautiful club with a head made of persimmon, and I hit it beautifully, straight down the middle. I hadn't noticed that the fairway canted some toward the pond, but of course it did. My ball discovered this fact immediately, however, and followed the slope and gravity toward the water.

Naturally I yelled at it to stop, but, like a thirsty horse racing for the watering hole, it ignored me completely. After what appeared to be a joyful run, it rolled happily into the pond.

This was, of course, completely unfair. I had hit the perfect shot and had been rewarded (punished, really) with a terrible result. Anger swelled up within me, and as one of my family was saying, sincerely, "Oh, that's too bad," I took my golf club by the handle and attempted to fling it down the fairway after that miscreant ball.

If a golf shot hit in anger is not likely to go where you intend, neither is a club thrown in anger. At least this one didn't, because somehow I managed to throw it over the fence to the left of the tee box and into the trees and shrubbery.

Now I was angry and embarrassed, and I had potentially lost one of my favorite clubs. I went over to the fence to see if I could see it, and I could. It was in a tree, grabbed by the branches. I climbed the fence and saw that I was lucky indeed, because the tree was tall but was growing on the side of a hill. I could still reach my club with another club. And I did, retrieving it and discovering that the club was unhurt while my body was apparently unscathed. All was well.

But that night I started on a three-day lesson that I have

never forgotten. It began when I noticed my legs itched.

In the process of getting my club out of the tree I had (while wearing golf shorts) been standing in a large patch of poison oak, and the plant had lived up to its name.

I have been angry on the golf course since that time, but not often. Because every time that anger rears its ugly head, my whole body starts to itch.

Do not let anger master you on the course. You may not get poison oak, but the anger itself is poison enough.

Embarrassment

Have you ever hit a bad golf shot with other people watching? Of course you have, and you have probably been a little embarrassed by it. All of the best players in the world, both current and past, have done exactly the same thing.

In a President's Cup match in San Francisco, I was just twenty feet from Phil Mickelson when he hit a 40 yard pitch shot 25 yards. Chunked it. This is the same Phil Mickelson who has sold tens of thousands of videos on the short game, the same Phil Mickelson who is always mentioned when TV announcers play the "who-has-best-short-game" game.

In the 2013 U.S. Open, with millions of people watching on TV and online, Steve Stricker, one of the best ball strikers of his era, shanked a long iron about 50 yards right and out-of-bounds. This was made worse by the fact that it was his fourth shot on the par five, as he had already hit his drive out-of-bounds.

Was he embarrassed? Of course he was, and so was Phil when he chunked that pitch shot. Making an obvious mistake in front of a crowd, whether you're making a speech, acting in a play, or hitting a golf ball, causes a natural visceral reaction of personal discomfort in almost everyone. Often blood rushes to your face, making it turn red, and you can even be embarrassed by that.

Here's the difference between the great players like Phil and Steve and the not so great players, like most of us: the poor shot did not create another poor shot. I've been embarrassed by a poor shot, let it affect my psyche, and followed it up with another poor shot—sometimes on a later hole when facing the same kind of shot. Perhaps you have too.

The reason for all this is faulty logic, and once you get that squared away embarrassment may happen but will no longer wreak havoc with your score.

Here is the flawed syllogism: I play golf relatively well; people like me; therefore people must like me because I play golf relatively well. The dark side of buying into that error is that when you make a mistake, you think people no longer like you.

Here is the truth: except perhaps for an occasional opponent or a strong fan of your opponent, everyone watching you hit a golf ball wants you to do well. Likewise if you are singing in front of a crowd or making a speech, those in the audience want you to succeed. Virtually everyone is pulling for you, they are not sitting idly by waiting to judge you harshly as a person based on your performance.

If people like you, and I'll bet they do, it has nothing to do with your ability to play golf or the piano or deliver a line on stage. Those things might be used to justify their admiration, but they are not the cause of it—you are.

The emotion you want to feel when you miss a shot you should normally make is not embarrassment, it is surprise.

The more confidence you have in your game, in your ability to hit any particular shot, the more you will understand that it is an unusual thing for you to hit it badly. If it is not unusual for you to miss that shot, then you probably aren't embarrassed by missing it this time. The more quickly you accept this occurrence as the exception, the more quickly you will put it out of your mind and the better you will focus on the next shot.

Yes, I know that is easier to write than it is to do, because I've been there. So practice the shots you struggle with and do so under social pressure, not just financial pressure.

The alternative to that is to make the rest of the world disappear when you play, because if they aren't there you can't be embarrassed by what you do. Ben Hogan was so adept at that that he apparently failed to notice when his fellow competitor, Claude Harmon, made a hole-in-one on number 12 at the Masters.

If that fits your personality and you learn to do it, embarrassment will no longer be an issue. Getting a social game together, on the other hand, might be.

Incorrect focus

Every person who has played the game has been guilty of focusing on the wrong thing when hitting a golf shot. Personally speaking I feel like I've dodged a swift kick to the shin when I have incorrect focus and don't hit a poor shot, and I know I deserved it when the shot is less than it could be.

So what should I focus on? Basically, the target. There are a few reasons why I don't focus properly, but I find the primary reason the target isn't in my mind is this: I don't have a target.

Oh, sure, I look in the general direction of the fairway or the green or the hole, depending on what kind of shot is called for, and I might even pick out an aim point, but that is not the same as having a target. If I tried to kiss my wife as carelessly as I sometimes hit a drive, I'd be lucky to hit her face let alone her lips.

You've heard a lot about having a pre-shot routine, I'm sure. One great benefit is that your routine should always include the acquisition of a target. Whether you keep it in mind or not is another story, but at least you'll have one.

The old line "aim small miss small" is just as true in golf as it is in hunting. Make your target as precise as you can, because the smaller you make it the easier it is to focus on and the closer you will come to hitting it.

For me a target for a drive can be beyond where the ball will land, and on long shots usually is. A distant tree branch, steeple, flag, mountain, or high-rise will do if they happen to be available. Airplanes tend to move, so I'd probably stay away from those as targets. In links golf such targets are often not available, unless there is a slow moving cloud on the right line, so you may have to select a spot on the ground. If so, make it a small area of ground and not "the fairway" itself.

One of the reasons St. Andrews is more challenging than it might appear to be, by the way, is that the different kinds of grasses in different shades of yellows and greens that grow on that course make depth perception difficult and therefore make target acquisition a real art. Even in modern courses you'll find clever architects doing the same kinds of things to mess with your eye. What a great game we play!

A target for an approach shot, a pitch shot, a bunker shot or a chip shot should be a spot on the ground (ideally on the green) where you want the ball to land.

A target for a putt should either be a spot on the green you want the ball to roll over, the edge of the cup where you want the ball to enter the hole, or in some cases a spot on the inside back of the cup you want the ball to hit.

But on every shot, in order to score the best you can, you must have a target. A very important part of having a target is that it gives you something to focus on, occupying your mind deeply enough that you cannot focus on other things.

What else would you focus on? How about that tip you just saw the night before on TV? How about the instructional article you just read in a golf magazine? How about that position of the club you heard explained in an Internet video lesson?

Believe it or not I'd rather have you thinking about what you're going to have for dinner rather than thinking about something to do with your swing that you haven't practiced. At least in that case you have the chance of your instincts taking over and allowing you to hit a good shot.

Ideally you will hit your shots focusing on where to hit the ball. The antithesis is a focus on how to hit the ball. If you find yourself standing in address position thinking about how, back away and re-focus on the target. Thinking about how invariably leads to a bigger how many.

By all means watch the golf tips on TV, read the magazines, and try to learn from every source you can. But do not think about those things while you are trying to hit a golf ball on the course for a score unless you have practiced them and have some comfort level with them. Driving range? Sure. Practice round? No problem. Social game with your buddies? OK. Scoring round? Target.

Incorrect thinking

I remember a round in California where my friends and I got to talking about thinking too much. Someone even suggested that having a mind that was too bright might be detrimental to playing well. Of course we were really just trying to justify our own failings by making ourselves "overqualified" for the game. It's interesting that we could justify hitting poor shots by implicitly bragging about ourselves. Fortunately the conversation didn't last long—we weren't as smart as we pretended to be, but we were smart enough to know we were being pretty silly.

Still, Jack Nicklaus once said, "If you're thinkin' you're stinkin'," and a lot of people understand there is something to that. But it is one of those quotes you don't want to take out of context.

Thinking—and the Golden Bear would agree—is a healthy thing on a golf course. The secret is to think at the right time about the right things. Getting that one aspect right will not only make your score better, it will make you feel much better about the round. I wish I could explain that phenomenon more clearly, but it is invariably true.

Thinking should begin well before you reach the course, assuming you want to shoot a good score. This doesn't need to be deep or long, but it should set the stage for a good round. Think about the course, assuming you have played it before, and about one of your best playings of each hole. Have you made a birdie or an eagle on it, or a very good par? Have you hit a particularly fine drive or approach? Remember those shots for each hole on the course. You can do that the night before you play or while you are on your way to the course.

That little exercise will put you in a proper frame of mind to start the day, and it acts as a barrier for negative thoughts that want to creep in along the way. Positive emotional memories are amazing things. They help your psyche in several different ways, including getting you on the path of positive thinking for the day. And Dr. Norman Vincent Peale showed over and over in sermons and books the amazing power of positive thinking.

When you get to the range, think about the day and the weather and the company and the beauty of the game and its setting. Think about the joy of striking a ball well. Think about the shots you'll want that day, whether those are fading drives or high approach shots, and hit a few of those on the range.

On the practice green, think about the speed of the green. Hit a few putts of 40 to 60 feet in length, then make several putts from inside four feet and think what a great putter you are.

When you are headed to the first tee, think about the joy it is to get to play golf and to be able to play well. Not everyone has those privileges, and you should be thankful for them. This is what I call "broad" thinking and it is an excellent exercise between shots.

When it is your turn to hit, your thinking should become much more focused. Before we go into greater depth about all that, get these ideas firmly in mind:

- thinking starts pre-round (before you get to the course) and finishes post-round
- the farther you are from hitting a shot, the broader your thinking should be
- the closer you are to hitting a shot, the narrower your thinking should be
- when it is time to execute a shot, thinking fades into pictures, feelings, or actions that trigger the swing

Yes, there is thinking after the shot as well—and sometimes verbal commentary that is really more emotive than thoughtful. But the idea is that your thinking breathes in and out, becoming broader and narrower throughout the round. Now use your mind for some fun and think of at least three different ways to punctuate these words: I think I golf I think.

Fear

There are two kinds of fear that are common in tournament golf: fear of failure and fear of success. The latter is not as common as the former, but it is more common than people who love success imagine.

It is beyond the scope of this book to delve deeply into these fears, and I cannot offer a complete cure, but I want everyone reading to know that these are real fears and can cause real problems in people's lives.

The first time I encountered fear of failure was many years ago during my days as a tennis pro. One of my students

129

was playing in an indoor junior tournament of some status, and I was there to watch her. As I walked down the hallway toward the viewing area for the court she was on I passed a junior player, a boy, who was talking on a pay phone (I said it was many years ago) and crying. Being a responsible adult I stopped to see if I could help this young man, and while I was waiting it became apparent from his side of the conversation that he was (a) talking to his father, (b) reporting that he had lost his match, and (c) very afraid of his father's reaction to that news.

I didn't know what to do, although I did know what I wanted to do—make that father afraid of me. But all I could do was try to console the boy after he hung up, and I did a poor job of that.

So fear of failure can be present because real consequences for failure have been promised and perhaps even demonstrated in the past. And in my experience this particular fear almost always involves someone else whom we want very much to please, or someone we do not want to displease.

Fear of success can have outside players as well, but it can just as easily be a demon we carry completely on our own. Generally it is a by-product of having some success, then thinking that the pressure is always on to create more and more and more success. That brings with it more responsibility and (this is critical for many) the perception that expectations of you are constantly rising.

People who have this brand of fear often undermine their own chances to succeed further because it is not bearable to them to have to carry the weight of those expectations. I have heard David Feherty say he thinks that may have been one reason why his own golf game began to falter, and if that is his opinion it is probably correct.

While I have had some training in counseling and have worked with some people who have had debilitating fear, there is little I can write here that will help someone specifically. I still think about that kid in the hallway crying on the phone and wonder whatever happened to him. Odds are he quit playing tennis, which is a shame.

What I can do is give a couple of broad pieces of advice that might be useful, and recommend that if your fear is so great that these don't make a dent in it, that you should see a counselor who can help you with your particular situation.

The first thing you have to do is acknowledge the fear. Face it and it often diminishes in size, like the Wizard of Oz, who turned out to be a little man behind a big machine. We have great imaginations, and we often give our fears power they don't really possess. The challenge is, rational words and thoughts are almost powerless against them because fears mostly reside in our emotions.

A psychologist friend of mine once worked with one of my tennis clinic groups and asked them what they were most afraid of. He then supplied his own picture of birds flying down suddenly from the sky and pecking his eyes out. Then he said, "Compared to that, losing my next tennis match is hardly worth being afraid of." He said if you face your fear with a comparative picture in mind, you'll begin to see that it is not so big.

In fact the Bible even says not to fear man, who can only kill you, but to fear the one who can destroy both your body and your soul. Not that you want to be killed, but even there you might say that this is not the worst that could happen. Look straight at it, keep it in perspective, and your fear will be much smaller than you think of it now.

For a while I suffered from, as an adult, a fear of big dogs. I fed it in the ways people do, imagining all kinds of things including the "fact" that the dogs could smell my fear and were therefore likely to attack. As if all dogs that reach a certain size are predators. Then one day I found myself alone at my brother-in-law's house with his big, strong, German shepherd. It was summer, so I got into the pool in an effort to avoid the dog, who then came out to the pool either to maul me or to play. I had nowhere to go and had to face my fear, which of course turned out to be unfounded, and my fear of big dogs began that day to shrink and today has completely turned around.

Which leads me to the second bit of advice, and that is to replace the fear with love. This is quite biblical itself, because 1 John 4:18 starts out "There is no fear in love: true love has no room for fear." In context John is talking about the final judgment, but it is applicable to much of life, including golf.

Are you afraid of bunker shots? Learn to love bunker shots. Are you afraid of short putts? Learn to love short putts. Are you afraid of winning? Learn to love winning and dismiss the baggage that comes with it. Are you afraid of losing? Do not learn to love losing, but learn to love yourself even when you lose the match, and learn to love the lessons you learn in losing that will help make you better.

Here is one more bit of advice about fear from a fellow we think of as extraordinarily brave. It is a quote from Theodore Roosevelt, who, as a young man in the 1880's moved to the then-rugged West from a life of relative ease in the East. He said, "When I got there there were all kinds of things I was afraid of. Snakes, bears, gunfighters, etc. But I pretended not to be afraid, and after a while it turned out I wasn't."

Interesting advice from a man who went on to lead the Rough Riders.

* * *

PUTTING IT INTO PLAY

How do you make your mind your friend in golf? First you have to have a word with it. Sit down with your mind and tell it how much you appreciate it, especially that it keeps you breathing and keeps your heart beating without even being asked to do so. Honor it for making you clever on occasion and wise sometimes, and for having the sense to get you somehow into the game of golf.

Then explain to it that while it is amazing and wonderful and powerful, it can only have control insofar as you allow it. You are the boss, and you want your mind to work for you and with you, not independently. Let it know that you will be monitoring it and that if it begins to slip into a mode that is not helpful you will be stepping in to correct that.

You might even say that you'll give it great freedom to create, and that you will listen to it when it advises you to hit an eight iron instead of a nine, and that you will apologize when it suggests a strategy that you override and find out you shouldn't have.

The truth is your mind is your mind, it is not a mind of its own, and it really is up to you to use some part of that mind (the will) to use the rest of your mind better. "Take every thought captive," the Good Book says, from which I infer that such a thing can be done.

Realize that almost every decision you make on a golf course will have some emotion attached to it, if not driving it. That is fine until you allow the emotions too much freedom. If you find yourself justifying an emotional decision (I'm going for the flag) with rational statements (I once hit a shot that would have worked here) rather than having your rational thoughts simply agree with the emotion, recognize that you are potentially in trouble, stop, and call out the emotion to stand on its own. Pure emotions almost never can.

The fact is, you can decide to make your mind an asset on the golf course. Those who make that decision and then use their mind well will consistently perform at a higher level than those who don't.

12

Hate Bogeys As Much As You Love Birdies

Every golfer, from the best in the world to the occasional player, loves to make a birdie. Beating "Old Man Par," as Bobby Jones called him, is delightful even for one hole. Beat him for a whole round and a celebration is in order.

A common scorekeeping custom is to draw a circle around each birdie on the card, and it's fun to see those. It is also a custom to draw a square around a score that is a bogey, and a square around a square around the number if it is a double bogey. Or two circles if it is an eagle.

Doing that will help you add up your score quickly, because you can just count the circles and squares and know almost instantly how much over or under par you are for that round. (One of my phone apps that keeps score has all the pars in blue, all the birdies in red, and all the bogeys in green. Double bogeys are black and eagles are gold. It's the same concept, as you can see, but I still wish they had figured out how to make them circles and squares.)

My tendency is to look at the scorecard and focus on the circles. I like circles on my card, and I like saying I had two or three or four (or more) birdies. I don't like squares, and I don't like saying I had bogeys. But bogeys happen, and I have to own up to those just like I do the birdies.

One thing that has helped me score better is to have a subtle shift in my attitude about birdies and bogeys. I still love the one and hate the other, but now I hate bogeys more than I love birdies. Here's why.

If I make a bogey on the first hole and you make a par, you can go under par on the very next hole. I can't, because I have to make up for that bogey before I can think about getting under par. You have 17 holes in which you can go lower than par, and I have 16. If I don't make a "bounce back" birdie on two, I now only have 15 holes to get below par. If I also bogey two, I stand on the third tee with only 14 holes to get under par, because I have to use two of my remaining 16 holes just to get back to even.

Another way to say this is that every bogey costs me two holes—the one I made bogey on and the hole that I have to use to make up for the bogey—so I hate bogeys. The more I learn to hate them, the harder I try to avoid them. You should see me grinding over some of the par putts I have. I work so hard at them you'd think they were to win the U.S. Open, or at least the club championship. The truth is that I probably have more intensity on some pars than I do on some birdies. If I miss the birdie putt at least it doesn't cost me a hole.

My goal, by the way, is to also hate the bogeys I make in life. I have a tendency that may not be uncommon to laud my good works and ignore my failures, kind of like praising birdies and glossing over bogeys. But as I learn to hate bogeys in life I find that I behave a little better, just like I play a little better for hating bogeys on the course.

Don't get me wrong—you should love birdies. My friend Jeffrey makes birdies by the boat load, and consequently he has set several course records around the country. I asked him once about "going low" and he said the secret was to make a birdie and then want another birdie, and then another. "You can't have too many birdies in one round," he said, and I agree. Most of us will have a few birdies and then want to protect them, so we begin to play with some timidity. Not Jeffrey. Every birdie he makes, he believes, wants to have more circle friends on the scorecard.

But aggressively trying to make birdie on almost every hole is for the accomplished player. For a fellow with an Index of 15, there may only be four birdie holes on an eighteen hole course. For someone like Jeffrey, most courses have at least twelve birdie holes and some have more.

Think about your home course for a moment and count on the fingers of your right hand the holes where you think you should almost always have a birdie putt. On my former home course those would include 1, 3, 5, 6, 10, 11, 13, 15, 16 and 18. Notice that 2, 4, 7, 8, 9, 12, 14 and 17 are missing.

I have birdied each of those holes, but that doesn't make them birdie holes for me. Numbers 2, 4, 7 and 12 are the par three holes on that course, and in fact I birdied all four of those in a single round once. Still, I don't consider them birdie holes.

On the other side of the equation, I think of 8 and 12 as possible bogey holes. The fact is I have made bogey or worse on every hole on the course, but those are the only two (and they are the number 1 and 2 handicap holes) on which I think of a par as almost a birdie.

Take a moment and go over the holes on your course and decide if they are birdie, par, or bogey holes. Just the act of doing that will help you make an honest assessment of your own game, and that is a good thing.

You can even take a scorecard and circle the holes you think of as birdie holes and put squares around the holes you think of as bogey holes. Match those with your actual scores when you are done, and after a few rounds you will see which holes are being nice to you and which are not so nice.

Keep playing the first kind well, and think about how you play the others and see if another plan of attack is possible.

The point of doing this is to help you think realistically about your game and about each hole. You don't want to set your expectations too low, of course, but you also don't want to set them artificially high. Par may be par, but it may not be your par. Approach the course with this knowledge in hand and see if it helps both your attitude and your score.

* * *

PUTTING IT INTO PLAY

Back in the 1950's there was a joke where a fellow's wife suspected him of seeing another woman on a Sunday morning when he had been out, but he claimed to be innocent and said he had been at church.

She said, "If you were at church, what did the preacher preach about?"

"Sin," he replied.

"Oh, yeah," she continued, "What did he say about sin?"

"He was against it."

If you happen to go to a church some Sunday morning these days you aren't likely to hear a sermon on sin. Although most preachers are still against it, they rarely talk about it.

They tend to stay on the positive side and talk much more about love, which they are for. But only talking about love and only talking about birdies have a common problem: sin and bogeys are real and they need to be acknowledged and avoided.

I'm not suggesting that making a bogey is the equivalent of a sin, although some bogeys I've had should probably be classified as such, but it will be important for you to assign a great enough weight to a bogey that you'll go to great lengths to avoid having one.

Call it the name of something you do not want to have, something you hope to avoid, whether that is sin, a cold sore, a bad date, or a traffic ticket.

Just a little extra incentive is sometimes all we need to have the extra focus that will help us make par from a tough location.

However you learn to hate bogeys, reward yourself for every hole you play where bogey is in the picture and is still avoided. You'll be surprised at how quickly your scores will start coming down!

Note: I've shared this verbally with friends of mind who have said, "I think bogeys are fine. It's double-bogeys I can't stand." If in fact your goal is to break 90 rather than to break 80 or 70, that is absolutely true, and the thoughts above should be applied to your game as they are appropriate.

If a bogey is your par, even on some holes, be happy to get one there. But every time you make a bogey you might say to it, "I'm happy to see you today, Mr. Bogey, but one day soon you'll have to clean up, brush your hair, stand up straight and turn yourself into a par."

13

Playing With KASH

Years ago I was the General Manager of an athletic club, and in that role I attended a management training course in Chicago with several of my fellow General Managers from the same company. While a number of managers don't like that sort of thing, I embrace it. There is always more to learn and there are always new ways of thinking. It didn't hurt that I got to hang out with some of my friends and that the instructor was engaging and occasionally funny.

One management "formula" he taught us was not new, but it was presented in a catchy acronym that was easy to remember—KASH. Later I used it often in hiring, but it can be used for training (its original purpose), for evaluations, and even for disciplinary interviews. We can even use it for golf.

The four elements are Knowledge, Attitude, Skills, Habits.

In most interviews at most companies, most questions are either directly or indirectly about knowledge and skills. If I happened to be interviewing someone for the role of aerobics instructor, for instance, I might ask her/him about different approaches to aerobic training, and I might ask to see a demonstration of their skills by having them lead a class with no people and then one with some advanced and some beginning students. If the knowledge and skills were strong, that candidate would be on the short list.

Habits are almost never discussed in interviews, it seems to me, and I've been on both sides of the desk many times. We'll come back to that.

Attitude is something we do look for in interviews, but we often don't probe it. We sense it, we have a gut feeling for it, we like the person or don't like the person, and we get all around the edges of attitude but we rarely go deep there.

The interesting thing about all that is that knowledge and skills are the easiest things to teach and alter, habits themselves can be changed but usually not quickly, while an underlying attitude is almost impossible to change, and yet is the most important aspect of the four elements!

So how does that apply to your golf game? My guess is that you spend the vast majority of your "golf improvement" time working on knowledge and skills. I do not deny their importance, and a lot of this book is about knowledge and skills, but they may be less critical to good scores than habits and attitude.

Let's take a look at each one in turn and think about how to apply them for optimal results.

Knowledge

You are reading this book, so you are acquiring knowledge. Since this is not the first golf book you've read, lets characterize you as an acquirer of golf knowledge. Good for you! You want to know more and you believe that knowing more can be and will be beneficial to your score. I agree. So where do you get it, and how do you discern whether or not it is useful knowledge?

Golf knowledge is available everywhere. TV, Internet, books, pros, driving ranges, golf courses, pamphlets, manufacturers, sporting goods stores and magazines are all places you might find golf knowledge.

Often this takes the form of "tips" on golf, pithy pieces that are easy to assimilate and possibly even easy to incorporate into your game. Most of this golf knowledge is about how to hit a ball, but it ranges from that to course architecture to games you can use to bet with while you are playing. For now let's limit our discussion to how to hit a chip shot.

I would define "chip shot" for you, but whose definition do I use? One famous player says a chip shot is a short shot, normally made close to a green, in which you use the leading edge of the club to hit the ball. For years I defined it as a short shot that was in the air for less than half the distance to the hole and rolled most of the way.

Likewise I defined a pitch shot as one that flew in the air farther than it rolled on the ground, while our famous pro defines a pitch as a shot in which you use the bounce of the club when you are hitting the ball. (Obviously it is the face of the club that hits the ball, not the leading edge—unless you hit it thin—or the bounce. But you get the idea.)

My point is that people don't even agree on the definition of these simple shots, let alone how to hit them. So what do you do when the knowledge you are gathering conflicts with knowledge you already have, or with the knowledge offered by another Master Instructor whom you greatly admire?

What I've decided for myself is to read as much as I can, even if the advice from one person seems to contradict the advice from another person, but not to try to apply that knowledge to my own game unless it does not cause a conflict with what I'm already doing that works well.

In other words, having that knowledge in my head is just fine because some day it may be useful, but unless it is easily applicable to my game I leave it in the world of understanding and don't let it in to the world of application.

For example, Phil Mickelson (amazing short game) uses a theory called "hinge and hold." James Sieckmann, short game guru to many Tour pros, advocates releasing the club through the shot. Which do I use? The one that is easiest to put into my game. But I remember the other one because some day it may prove to be useful.

Knowledge is powerful. Get it and use it, but don't stop there.

skills

Want a deft touch around the green? Want to putt like Brad Faxon? Want to "bend it like Bubba?" Those are skills, and we golfers spend a lot of time thinking about and trying to improve and add to our skills. Even though we sometimes go about that in less than productive ways, our skills do grow and that makes the game more fun and more challenging. Keep working on skills, honing those you have and adding to them as you have the time and opportunity.

Habits

Effective habits applied to golf can be very beneficial, both in the practice realm and during a round. The place where this is most obvious is in a pre-shot routine, but it shows up in other places as well.

The popular answer to how long it takes to form a habit is 21 days, and undoubtedly it is possible to form some habits in that length of time. Research indicates that the more complex a habit is, however, the longer it will likely take to make it stick.

So how complex is having a pre-shot routine, and how hard is it to have one of those be part of your game? And is it worth it? That last was a rhetorical question. The answer is a resounding yes.

You already know that a pre-shot routine is very important, and if you read Chapter 5 you know you have one. Have you made it purposeful and valuable? I hope so.

Whether or not you have worked on it, you have a pre-shot routine. So do your golf buddies, regardless of your skill levels. And your pre-shot routine, even if you haven't taken time with it, is good for you. Somehow it helps you get set to hit a golf shot, and when you change that routine significantly it may adversely affect the outcome of the shot you want to hit.

You can prove this to yourself by simply observing your friends the next time you play. There is no need to look for or document any particular specifics, just watch. After the third or fourth shot that a player takes, you'll begin to recognize a pattern that will include timing (e.g. how long it takes them to hit a shot once they are set up to it), sequence (which hand do they grab the club with first, which foot sets up first, do they take a practice swing (or seven), etc.), and alignment (do they start behind the ball or beside the ball, when and how do they check their alignment), and possibly some personalized movements, like a forward press, a cocking of the head, or a tightening of the grip.

I wouldn't recommend that you change the elements of your pre-shot routine without thinking through it, but I would recommend that you make sure it contains everything you need to hit the best shot you can hit.

Your pre-shot routine must become a habit for you if you wish to play your best.

There is much more to habits in golf than the pre-shot routine. My goal here in that regard is simply to get you to be more aware of those habits, and then decide if they are beneficial or detrimental to your game. The answer isn't always obvious.

Attitude

I've saved the most critical of the four KASH elements for last. And I call it the most critical for one simple reason: it is. Attitude affects everything.

While my focus as a pastor was often on the soul, you may

know that the Bible has a lot to say about the mind. Lest you think of that as merely a reference to the intellect, the term heart is also used a lot and often combined with mind, as in "Love God with your whole heart and mind." Think of the heart as your emotions, combine that with your rational self, and you've pretty much got the whole person.

So I've done a fair amount of talking with people about their hearts and minds, including talking to my very own self, and often (in both cases) because of an apparent loss of control of one or the other.

The same is true on the golf course, except there I've done more talking to myself than to others about getting control of the "heart and mind." The key to that, I believe, is attitude.

I can currently think of several post-round interviews of winners on various golf tours in which "attitude" was either the direct or indirect answer to the question, "What made the difference this week?"

Did these people suddenly develop skills they had never had? Of course not. Habits? No. New knowledge? Not that they admitted. The difference was a better attitude, and that attitude allowed them to use the habits, knowledge and skills they possessed in a manner that was much more effective and efficient.

There is no need to belabor this point, because even a cursory (honest) examination of your own attitude on days you've played extraordinarily well compared to days when you've played below expectations will reveal it.

The question is, What can you do about it?

One wag said there were two ways to change your atti-tude and make it stick: deep religious conversion or a frontal lobotomy. I think it's a little more subtle—and a little more doable—than that. At least when it comes to golf.

Attitude and Zzzzzzz..

The first and simplest way to adjust your attitude is to make sure you have enough sleep. You'd be amazed at the number of arguments, accidents and angry words that can be traced back to sleep deprivation. You want world peace? A great place to start would be to require all world leaders to sleep a minimum of seven hours a night. Want to have a more civil dialogue in congress—or even with your spouse? Make sure it is conducted when everyone has had plenty of shuteye.

Specialists can and have written volumes on this, but none of them have said it any more eloquently than a long-time professor at Stanford University who gave his students extra credit if they fell asleep in class. (When he retired, hundreds of former students and even the Stanford band showed up in the lecture hall wearing pajamas.)

University students aren't the only sleep-deprived segment of the population, they are just less aware of it than many because they are young and invincible. Odds are that you are at least somewhat sleep deprived yourself, and that is a bad thing for your attitude and, therefore, your golf scores.

Attitude and Perspective

OK, so your golf score is important to you. It's unlikely that you'd be reading a book like this if you didn't care what you shot. Golf may even be your livelihood, or a significant contributing factor to your livelihood, though for most of us it is not. Regardless of how important you perceive it to be, it's healthy to step back every once in a while and get a little different perspective.

Golf, for instance, is not as important as breathing.

It is not even as important as food, family, faith, or friends. Health trumps golf, at least in most cases. Your character is a bigger deal than your average score, integrity is more precious than par, and the difference between being a selfless servant and a selfish so-and-so is bigger than the difference between 69 and 70.

Although we hate to admit it, golf is a game. As I have said many times, golf is not life-and-death, it is more important than that. But I say that sarcastically, or at least I try to.

In true-confession style allow me to admit that I have put golf above all of the things I mentioned above, except breathing. But that one probably only escaped because I can do both at the same time without conflict.

When golf has been given a priority in my life that it does not merit, I do not get the best out of life or my game. So why do I do that?

Because I think my identity is wrapped up in whether or not I win. I think I am liked or not liked based on my scores because I treat myself that way. I love myself if I break par and hate myself if I shoot 76. This is not a healthy relationship.

The other side of that coin is caring too little about our score. Golf requires focus, and we tend not to focus well, if at all, on things we don't care about. (Indeed, being able to filter out those things that are irrelevant to a golf shot—things you don't care about—is a very useful skill.)

This idea of "caring too little" usually manifests itself in a situation where we have "given up" on a hole, or even a round. It is not a pretty picture, and it almost never results in a better score.

But what do you do? And I ask the question because this is one of the most challenging situations you'll encounter on a golf course, especially in competition. I have an answer, but it is far from being an easy answer.

Let's say you are playing in a two-day tournament that has flights determined by the first day of play, and your goal is to make it into the championship flight. You know you'll have to shoot no more than two over par (we'll call that 74) to achieve your goal.

Now let's say you come to number 15, an average par four, and you are already three over par. You have this hole, then a par five, then a tough par four, and finally a reachable par four at 18. And because as you tee up on 15 you are thinking that you only need one birdie in the last four holes instead of thinking about your shot, you line up wrong and hit your drive out of bounds.

Since score and not shot was already in your mind, it is but the work of an instant to say the best you can hope for is to be four over after this hole, which means you need two birdies in three holes to shoot 74.

And because you are still calculating all that and still living in the future rather than the present, you make double on 15, meaning you now need to birdie in.

You stand on the tee of the par 5 telling yourself you have eagled this hole in the past and you can do it again, and in spite of your hope you make par. Here is where you can "care too little" and come in not with a 76, but with a 78. Now you are in danger of not only missing the championship flight, but also the first flight.

Do you care? Not outwardly, where you simply go about your business, but inwardly you know that you gave up before the round was over, and if the score doesn't convict you of being something of a quitter, your own conscience will.

For many years on the PGA Tour (where the prize money is extraordinarily high), players have been accused of playing for the money instead of playing to win. Then along came one Eldrick "Tiger" Woods, and things changed.

Tiger, a polarizing figure because of his boorish behavior on the course and his (admittedly) immoral behavior off the course, all while playing the most extraordinary golf many of us have ever seen, changed the rules. Or at least he brought them into focus.

Not only was Tiger the best golfer on the planet, he was the last player on the planet to give up on his game by pretending not to care. On the first green or the 72nd green, whether he was ten shots ahead of the field or ten behind the leader, Tiger put full effort into every shot.

More true confession time. I have done that less than five times in my life, and Tiger did it round after round after round. Is that a habit I could learn?

I suppose it still happens that some Tour players will occasionally find themselves somewhere in the final round with no chance to win and "mail in" their score. You won't see those players on TV though, because those guys who have a chance to win are working on every shot.

Imagine how your own game would improve if you didn't

give up on a round just because you had one bad hole. Imagine how much better you would feel about yourself for fighting back in any way you could from a double or triple bogey. Imagine how much more prepared you'd be for competition if you stayed focused on your game even when you played socially. Imagine being Tiger Woods on the golf course—or even Ben Hogan—and making every shot count.

Try it for one round. You won't be able to do it, but try it anyway. Then try it again and again and again until one day you play a round of golf where you can honestly say that you gave 100% of your attention to every shot you hit, including tap-ins that were less than one foot in length.

Learn how to never give up on a single shot, even if you are having a poor scoring day, and see what it does for you and your score.

Guaranteed it will make you sleep better, not just because it is physically demanding and mentally exhausting, but because it is good for your soul.

* * *

PUTTING IT INTO PLAY

Byron Nelson was a man who played professional golf for fourteen years in the 1930's and 1940's, and a few times after that. He won 54 sanctioned events, including five majors, and in 1945 he won eighteen tournaments, including an astounding, amazing, never-to-be-repeated, eleven (11!) tournaments in a row.

I could go on and on with statistics and facts about his accomplishments on the course, but when you hear anyone who knew him (he died in 2006) talk about Mr. Nelson (which is what most called him, out of respect) they talk about his character.

In 1974, almost three decades after he retired from playing professional golf, he was honored with the highest award the USGA grants, the Bob Jones award. In 2000 he was the first recipient (along with Arnold Palmer and Jack Nicklaus) of the Payne Stewart award, and in 2006 he was awarded a Congressional Gold Medal. Yes, his accomplishments on the course gave him a platform and visibility, but his conduct both on and off the course was his primary legacy. And he appreciated that.

Few people will ever match the number of wins Nelson had or the number of majors he won, and it is extraordinarily unlikely that anyone will ever match his winning streak, but all of us can try to play with KASH, as he did.

As a young man Nelson played with wooden shafted clubs, but as he was entering the professional game steel was taking over. He had to acquire knowledge about these clubs and how they could be used most effectively, and he did.

After one particular season early in his career, he realized his performance from the bunkers had been very poor, so he spent hours and hours in the off-season practicing from the sand and increasing his skill level. He did that with any part of his game that needed it.

Byron's goal (unspoken for a number of years) was not to play golf tournaments forever, it was to be a rancher. He played golf because he was extraordinarily skilled at it, and because it gave him an opportunity to earn money to buy a ranch. He therefore developed the habit of meticulously keeping records of his earnings, his expenditures, his scores, his statistics (like sand saves), and any other information that would help him achieve his goal sooner.

And his attitude on and off the course was a model for us all. Ken Venturi, himself a member of the World Golf Hall of Fame, described Byron this way:

"As a competitor, Byron was able to be mean and tough and intimidating—and pleasant. You can always argue who was the greatest player, but Byron is the finest gentleman the game has ever known."

Want to play golf for cash? Then you'd better learn to play the game with KASH, and there is no one better to emulate than Mr. Nelson.

14

Results

Back when I was a preacher I often spoke about getting out of "the results business." "Be who you are supposed to be," I would say, "and do what you are called to do. Then leave the results to God."

This is a little tricky for us golfers because we all have a tendency to measure ourselves by results. "How many wins have you had," we ask.

Have you noticed that few ever ask about how many losses we've had, as though they are inconsequential? How silly! In golf, results are expressed varyingly as: Points race. Money race. Driving distance. Greens in regulation. Index. Fairways hit. Both pros and amateurs are bombarded with results—some of them disguised as "statistics"—every time they play. Even if the only result is something we call score, it is still a result.

Now I think it is a fine thing to keep score, and I think

that keeping track of a lot of other stats is also wise. In fact, understanding where you need improvement and where you are strong is a key component in helping you lower your scoring average (another result). Those things must be looked at objectively, though, just as Mr. Nelson looked at his sand-save numbers one year and knew it was a weakness for him that needed to be corrected.

So what about this "get out of the results business" talk?

Simply put it falls into two categories. The first and most important is that you should not define yourself by the results. Having a high score in golf does not make you a loser, and having a better score than your opponent does not make you a winner.

For instance, a young man I've never met (though I have met his father, who happens to be a PGA Class A professional) decided to turn pro. He had a solid junior and amateur career, played in college all four years, and wanted to take his game to the next level. So he declared himself a professional and started looking for places to play.

Within a short period of time he learned that there was a pre-qualifier to get into a qualifier to play in a PGA Tour event in West Virginia, not far from where he lives. So he entered, and he played well enough to get into the qualifier.

That made him one of a lot of people (perhaps a hundred) vying for a very few (perhaps four) spots in the tournament. And he made it. Sweet!

And then he shot something like fourteen over par for the first two days of the tournament and missed the cut by a million. Yet if you asked him about the whole experience, I guarantee you he would say he was a winner.

Blayne Barber was in the second stage of Q-School in

2013 and had made his way through to the finals, giving him a strong possibility of securing his card on the Tour. But he couldn't get it out of his mind that he might have brushed a leaf in a bunker on his backswing during his last round, even though the only other potential witness (his caddie and brother) swore that he had not touched it.

So he went to the officials and disqualified himself, because he could not go on playing with the thought that he may have turned in an incorrect card. If you only looked at the scores you would say that Barber did not win, but by every other measure the young man was clearly a winner.

To apply this to yourself in real time is an important skill, and, oddly enough, if you apply it correctly you will find that your golf scores will improve because of it.

Whether it is a single shot or a number on a scorecard at the end of a round or the end of a tournament, your golf performance does not define you. Results are just results, they are not you.

The second aspect of getting out of the results business that will help your game is equally important, and it is often called "staying in the moment." When we are concerned about results (the future) rather than the task at hand (the present), our golf game almost always suffers.

Have you ever stood over a shot and had the thought, "I wonder what _____ will think of me if I miss this?" Of course you have, and so have I. If you don't get that out of your mind before you hit, the odds are that you'll find the answer to your question very soon.

Of course the reverse is true as well, and Arnold Palmer tells the story of walking down the 18th fairway of a tournament already counting the victory. That adversely affected his play and the win he had counted on did not materialize. Thinking about results instead of playing the shot in front of him cost him the tournament.

One secret for keeping your focus off the end result and on the shot at hand is to never know where you stand. I wish I had known about that several decades ago when I was playing Mr. Cook in the club championship. But I was a teenaged hotshot golfer with a handicap of 2 (the Index hadn't been invented yet) and Mr. Cook was a grocery store owner with a handicap of 20.

This was a net match-play event, so I was giving a stroke a hole. That sounds like a lot, but the math was simple enough and I never had to wonder if we were playing a stroke hole or not, because every hole was a stroke hole. That meant that if we tied a hole he won it, and if I beat him by two or more strokes on a hole, I won it.

A brief aside: In matches like this the lower handicap player should win the majority of the time. I know that some folks think that isn't true because a high handicap might belong to a decent player who just has a "blow up" hole now and then. Maybe, but the USGA tracks these kinds of things and they show that the better player still wins most of the time.

Although I didn't know all that back then, I was pretty confident in my chances. Sure enough I was one hole ahead with one hole left to play (dormie), and all I had to do to win the match was to halve the last hole (beat Mr. Cook by one stroke). The final hole was a par five I could reach in two that he was unlikely to reach in three, and as we teed up I began wondering who I would play in the next round.

Sure enough I was on the green in two, and Mr. Cook was

about fifty yards short of the green in four with his ball lying in a small, dry depression. My putt, though fairly long, was a formality, and I watched with detached interest as Mr. Cook hit his fifth shot. I vaguely remember it landing just short of the green, bouncing on, and then rolling into the hole for the most unlikely par I could imagine.

Had I been tending to business I would have already had my putt lined up with the distance firmly in mind, but since I wasn't and I suddenly knew that I had only two putts instead of the three or four I'd calculated, I stepped up and three-putted for a five with considerable ease. Mr. Cook took his hole-out for par, his stroke for birdie, a win on the hole, a tie for the 18, and his brand new confidence to the first playoff hole, which he parred to win the match.

That answered my question about my next opponent with some finality.

Byron Nelson, the man who played with KASH, learned to not know where he stood in a tournament, whether it was match play or stroke play. Someone had to tell him at the end of each round what he had shot or whether or not he had won. Of course he kept a card in order to verify the scores, but he mastered the ability to refrain from adding it up along the way.

How can you do that? It takes some practice. Start by going around with a friend who will cooperate by keeping your score for you and promising to never talk about or ask about that score during the round. He or she can talk about the weather, the news, or even the shot at hand, but there can be nothing like, "You need this for a birdie," or "nice par." Make every shot an individual event, play that shot to the very best of your ability, and then move on to the next shot.

The results will take care of themselves.

* * *

If profit is your only goal in business you may achieve it, but you may also cut corners to get it, or even cheat just a little. It is easy when the result becomes your sole focus to say that the end justifies the means, which of course it does not. If the means can't justify themselves, they ought not be employed.

The same thing is true in golf. If score is your only goal, you may find yourself compromising your beliefs for a number. This is not a good idea.

It is a good idea, as Steven Covey wrote years ago, to begin with the end in mind. There is nothing wrong with saying, "Today I will shoot 65" and getting that message clearly to your very powerful mind, then thinking about how you will go about that. But once you get on the course and are following your game plan, which must include playing one shot at a time, the results will take care of themselves. Your score may well be a 65, but too much focus on that number can derail you, as I wrote in the chapter on knowing your score before you shoot it.

The result you ultimately want in golf is not a score, even though that can be fun and give you a sense of accomplishment. The result you want is satisfaction and joy. You want to be able to look back on the round you played and know that you enjoyed being there, that you enjoyed challenging yourself to improve, and that you enjoyed being challenged by the course and perhaps by an opponent to raise your level of play. You want to find satisfaction in your effort, and possibly in overcoming some part of the game that has troubled you in the past. Whether you won or lost and what you shot is ultimately far less important than satisfaction and enjoyment.

The most devastating round of golf I ever played was in a qualifier for the U.S. Senior Amateur. I was not mentally ready for that round of golf, although I had it on good authority from my pro that I was more than physically ready.

I made several mistakes coming into that event that added up to an almost perfect storm, and I had the worst round I had played since I could remember. The worse it got the worse I got, and I wanted more than anything to quit and walk off the course.

While it took me a long time to understand it, I derived satisfaction from that round because I did not quit. In fact I even corrected my scorecard, which had been added up a stroke low and would have given me a DQ instead of an official terrible score.

The sun still came up the next day, God and my wife still loved me, I still had gainful employment, and I could still play golf. Painful? Yes, it was, but while the apparent result was bad the real result turned out to be good.

It may seem odd to you that I'm finishing a book on how to lower your score not by cheering you on to incredibly good scores, but by saying that a lower score is simply the result of doing the right things on the course. Score is not a treasure you have to spend your life chasing, it is a result of doing the right things. Do those, and scratch will come to you.

Acknowledgments

Every piece of writing, especially one as lengthy as a book, owes a debt of gratitude to more people and experiences and books than the author will ever know. The greatest book of all time, the Bible, clearly has been the most influential book I've ever read, and I cannot recommend it highly enough. It is amazing to me how much there is in it that has actually helped my golf game. More importantly, it has helped my "life game" for eternity.

Our personal library numbers well over 2,000 books, and my golf collection alone is perhaps 15% of that. Which is telling when you consider that I have had several careers and have read widely in all of them. Golf was my first love in sports, and several of those books were published in the 1950's and 1960's—some far earlier.

I've read most of Bob Rotella's books, both of David L. Cook's fiction golf books (and have spent some time with him), and one of Lynn Marriott and Pia Nilsson's books (and have also met them, casually). Stan Utley's book titled *The Art of the Swing*, which is innovative in its use of private videos (you scan "tags" in the book to gain access) and is excellent in its ideas and instruction, is one I refer to often. I also once shared in a lesson from Stan with three others, and have recommended him as a pro to both professionals and amateurs.

Two other teachers whose books I go back to often are Jim Flick, whom I was fortunate to know a little, and Bobby Jones, one of the most elegant of writers as well as one of the best golfers ever. Harvey Penick's works are classic and not to be missed. Byron Nelson is one man I would loved to have known but didn't, and if I could pick anyone in time from whom to get a playing lesson it would be him.

You will have noticed influences from all of these and more in these pages, and I hope that I have represented them well and accurately.

My thanks also goes to Links Players everywhere, men and women who love the game of golf and gather in Fellowships to do life together, play golf together and get better at both together. I encourage you to find and join a Links Players Fellowship at your club, or start one if one doesn't currently exist, and I'll be happy to help you with that.

My fellow staff members at Links Players International are an inspiration to me both on and off the golf course. They all have made a positive difference in my life and in my game, and the national board of directors and my local board of advisers have both encouraged me as I have represented Links Players in Arizona. (One of those local fellows, Kim G., made the hole-in-one shown on the cover. I took the picture.)

Susan Mitchell is a good friend and fellow writer, as well as a member at a church where I was once the pastor. In spite of all that she graciously took much of her own time to help edit this work. Not being a golfer herself (though I introduced her to the game once upon a time), her perspective was particularly valuable. Her expertise and insights were extraordinarily helpful, and any writing errors that remain in this book are entirely mine.

My brother, Bill, was a golfer with an average handicap but an indomitable spirit of about a plus-7 (Tour quality). Although I was for years the better golfer, he made a hole-in-one before I did, and that was as it should be. He was the quintessential big brother, by miles and miles my favorite golf partner, and as I wrote this book I hoped that something in it would help his golf game. Unfortunately he passed from this life to the next during the time that I was writing. He approved of an early draft, though, and I hope he would have been pleased with the final product.

It was our father, George, who first put a golf club in my hands. Early on he saw that I had a natural talent for the game, and he encouraged me in ways I didn't even understand. Just thinking now about him introducing me to extraordinary golfers, taking me to tough courses, and telling me stories about the greats makes me smile. He helped me grow as a golfer and as a man, and it is the rare round of golf I play when I don't think of him.

My wife of more than four decades is not (yet) a golfer, but she would be (will be) a good one. I am blessed and amazed that she has put up with me for all these years. She has also encouraged me both in my golf, in my writing, and in every other endeavor I have taken on. Successful in her own busy life, she still finds the time to help me with whatever I am doing. In the process, she makes me a better me.

To all of these and many, many more, including everyone with whom I've been able to play this amazing game, thank you.

And thanks to you, the reader, for making the investment you have to obtain this book and read it. May God bless you, and may you get to scratch and beyond.

About the author

Lewis Greer once sat down on a curb in Seoul, South Korea, the city where he had first become a scratch golfer while stationed there with the U.S. Army, and made a no-strings-attached promise to God.

That the promise would ultimately lead to this book, or even to a role in golf, was beyond his imagination at the time. It still almost is.

Between then and now, Lewis has been a high-tech executive, a music company co-founder/owner, a tennis professional, a writer, and a pastor, among other things. Today he is the Arizona Region Director for Links Players International, a position that brings elements from his diverse past together in amazing ways.